The Nurse as Group Leader
Second Edition

Carolyn Chambers Clark, A.R.N.P., Ed.D., F.A.A.N., is an Advanced Registered Nurse Practitioner (A.R.N.P.) in Psychiatric/Mental Health Nursing and a Fellow of the American Academy of Nursing. She has conducted a private practice in group therapy and provided consultation for nurses in group work since 1966.

Dr. Clark (Ed.D., Teachers College, Columbia University) is a prolific contributor to nursing literature in the areas of psychiatric/mental health nursing, group processes, simulation gaming, teaching–learning, assertiveness, management, continuing education, and wellness. She is editor and publisher of *The Wellness Newsletter*. Her other Springer books include *The Nurse as Continuing Educator, Enhancing Wellness: A Guide for Self-Care,* and *Wellness Nursing: Concepts, Theory, Research, and Practice.*

The Nurse
as Group Leader
Second Edition

Carolyn Chambers Clark
A.R.N.P., Ed.D., F.A.A.N.

SPRINGER PUBLISHING COMPANY
New York

Springer Publishing Company, Inc.
536 Broadway
New York, NY 10012

87 88 89 90 91 / 5 4 3 2 1

Library of Congress Cataloging-in-Publication Data

Clark, Carolyn Chambers.
  The nurse as group leader.

  (Springer series on the teaching of nursing; v. 3)
  Includes bibliographies and index.
  1. Nursing services—Administration.   2. Leadership.
3. Small groups. I. Title. II. Series. [DNLM:
1. Group Processes—nurses' instruction.   2. Leadership—
nurses' instruction. W1 SP685SG   v.3 / WY   105   C592n]
RT89.C56   1987   362.1'73'068   87-4921
ISBN 0-8261-2332-5 (pbk.)

Printed in the United States of America

Contents

Preface to the First Edition

I decided to write this book when I was unable to locate a suitable text to use in a basic course in group dynamics. There were many texts on group psychotherapy and some books in the behavioral science areas that covered certain aspects of group skills and theory, but none was broad enough to cover the wide range of group situations within which nurses work; nor did they deal with the specifics of how to actually lead a group. Since the groups with which nurses become involved encompass nursing care planning groups, patient teaching groups, supportive groups for dying patients and their families, patient advocacy groups, and health team planning groups, it is essential that all nurses possess a knowledge of group processes and be proficient in assessment and intervention skills.

The Nurse as Group Leader is meant to fill the gap in nursing education texts by providing nurses with knowledge of how groups work and how to intervene to promote group movement. The word "leader" is used throughout the book to refer both to the nurse who is the formal or designated leader of the group and to the nurse who, while participating in a group, practices effective group skills to exert informal leadership of it.

Because the students I worked with seemed to learn both from group process recordings (with subsequent instructor feedback) and from simulated group experiences, I have given these two learning experiences equal treatment, with theory presentations in the text. Simulated exercises can be found at the end of each chapter, and sample recordings with instructor feedback are presented in Chapter 8.

This book is meant to be used by nursing students and graduate nurses in a variety of settings. It is my hope that upper-level basic nursing students, graduate students, and graduate nurses who work with groups will find the content useful in their efforts to improve their group skills. The book provides a general approach to the concepts of group work and its processes and thus is not designed for nurses majoring in mental health counseling, although it could be used as a supplemental text. It should be remembered also that this text is meant to be used by learners who already have the basic skills of interviewing and communicating in the one-to-one nurse–patient relationship.

Although the pronoun "she" is used throughout the text, the book is directed toward both male and female learners.

Carolyn Chambers Clark

Preface to the Second Edition

I have two reactions as I come back to *The Nurse as Group Leader*. The first is that my orientation to nursing has changed; it has become much more wellness- and systems-focused. The second edition of this book reflects this change. The second reaction is that the basic concepts, processes, and procedures are still relevant despite my change in orientation. The book reflects this reaction, too.

I believe the book has been strengthened by an enhanced focus on the following: team building, planned change, community organizational theory and skills, political and organizational theory and skills, and some new communication skills, including negotiation and confrontation. I have also added some simulations to strengthen leadership and communication skills.

As another decade of work with students, clients, and colleagues has passed, it has become clear to me that nurses need a thorough grounding in group skills and how to apply them, if they are to become effective leaders. This means actual experience in group leading in relatively nonstressful learning situations such as the simulated practice exercises included in this book. It is not enough to learn conflict and decision-making theory. Nurses at all educational levels must participate in real life or simulated group experiences if they expect to be confident, effective leaders.

Carolyn Chambers Clark
St. Petersburg, Florida, 1986

Acknowledgments

I wish to thank the many nurses and nursing students who have helped me learn about groups, especially students in the graduate program in Nursing at Pace University— Westchester, New York, and B.S.N. students at the University of Tampa, Florida, who shared in the development of the course, Group Dynamics and Leadership, upon which this book is based.

I also wish to thank my peer support group, Susan Di-Fabio, R.N., M.S., and Judith Ackerhalt, R.N., Ed.D., who helped me develop my own peer group skills.

C.C.C.

1
Introduction to Group Work

GROUPS ARE IMPORTANT

Groups are important to people from the moment they are born until their lives end. Socialization first takes place in the group called the family. Later, peer groups, social groups, religious groups, work groups, and political groups become important vehicles for learning and obtaining satisfaction.

The quality of peoples' lives often depends on their ability to perform effectively in the groups to which they belong. The nurse, as a social being, also belongs to many groups. The effectiveness of nurses in these groups depends on their ability to assess and intervene in the ebb and flow of processes that affect the internal workings of each group.

Group skills are important in nursing for at least two reasons. First, many tasks, such as planning for care, cannot be accomplished without the cooperation and collaboration of other health care givers. Nurses, therefore, need to learn to work effectively with their colleagues and with other health care personnel. Group skills in this kind of cooperation and collaboration are especially important now that nurses are striving to be recognized as peers by physicians, psychologists, social workers, and other health care professionals. Since the majority of nurses are women, the nursing profession is also faced with the necessity of working through nurse/doctor relationships; since most doctors are men, this involves working through male/female relationships. Effective group skills can assist nurses to be clear and assertive when working with various groups of health care personnel without resorting to aggressive or helpless behavior, withdrawal, or apathy.

Second, nursing functions include teaching and supportive assistance to clients and their families—two functions that can often best be provided within a group format. Such a format affords a number of experiences that the one-to-one nurse/client relationship cannot provide. Group experiences can also supply a more intense and different type of support; assistance in observing a wide range of responses; positive and negative feedback in a supportive way; pooling of resources and solutions to problems; knowledge that others share the same difficulty, fear, or anxiety; validation of one's own perceptions; and more efficient use of nursing time.

Group skills, then, are important to nurses not only when they form and lead groups that include clients or families but also when they are members of a planning or task group. In the latter case, nurses may or may not be designated leaders; if they are not, they can learn to provide *informal leadership* and thus help the group to function more effectively; in these cases, nurses become emergent or situational leaders. For the remainder of this book, the terms "leader" or "leaders" refer to both the designated and informal leaders.

THE GROUP AND SYSTEMS THEORY

The Group as a System

Systems theory provides an overriding theoretical framework for understanding and intervening in groups. A *theoretical framework* helps organize group information into an understandable whole. It provides categories to assist group leaders to organize their thoughts and observations. A framework is like a clothesline upon which group leaders can hang their observations in an organized manner. It provides a perspective or specific way of looking at what is happening in a group.

A group is a *system* because it has identifiable parts (members) yet is a whole entity (a group) with each part influencing each other part (if one member is angry, other group members will react to the anger). Systems also have *subsystems*. In groups, these are subgroups or pairs of individuals who cluster together around shared interests. The group is a whole and different from the sum of its parts; even if one group member remains silent throughout a group session, the group as a whole can achieve a goal; even if a group is composed of mature individuals, the group as a whole must struggle to be a mature group and develop ways to work together. Systems also have the property of openness and closedness; human systems are believed to be open systems, exchanging energy, matter, and information with their environment. Groups can be influenced by their environment too: For example, if the room is too warm, energy levels of group members may be low; if group leaders bring in handouts for the group there can be an exchange of information with the environment; and if group leaders serve refreshments from the cafeteria, matter from the environment (food) can be exchanged for energy. Systems have inputs (people, energy, information), throughputs (what goes on in the group), and outputs (products, such as decisions that are carried out between group meetings, influence on interactions outside of the group). A system has interactive parts: the leader influences the group members and vice versa. Leaders and group members are continually influencing each other, even when there is silence in the group.

From a systems point of view, growth occurs in a unidirectional fashion; a group does not reverse itself or regress; some behaviors or sessions may seem nonconstructive, but eventually, the group will move forward if the leader exerts helpful leadership behaviors.

Open systems show a regularity and predictability; observant group leaders will begin to notice behavior patterns in specific groups. In one group, every time one of the group members speaks, a silence may follow, or laughter or encouragement.

Living systems have these common elements, but they also have their unique patterns; no two groups are the same; there are processes that occur, but each group may display them in unique ways (Tappen, 1983, pp. 3–13).

Using systems theory can enable the nurse group leader to view group problems as systems issues, not as personal attacks or attitude problems, but as patterns that have been developed and are maintained by the system. In other words, many of the system problems discussed in Chapter 3 are best viewed as patterns that serve a purpose for the group. This does not mean that a pattern cannot be disrupted; suggested interventions for system pattern change are found in Chapters 3 and 4.

TYPES OF GROUPS

Nurses work primarily in three types of groups: task groups, teaching groups, and supportive or therapeutic groups. Table 1-1 lists the types of groups with which nurses most often work, their primary purposes, and examples of groups belonging to each type.

Task Groups

The primary purpose of *task groups* is to accomplish a given task; they place high priority on decision making and problem solving. Health care planning committees, nursing service committees, nursing teams, nursing care conference groups, hospital staff meetings, community organizational meetings, and Nurses for Political Action meetings are all examples of task groups in which nurses may participate (see Table 1-1).

Task groups are often formed to solve a given problem; for example, how can the consumer have input into health

TABLE 1-1 Types of Groups Amenable to Nurse Leadership

Group Type	Primary Purpose	Examples
Task	Accomplishing the task	Curriculum committee meeting Nursing service planning committee Nursing team meeting Nursing care conference Hospital staff meeting Community organizational meeting Nurses for Political Action meeting
Teaching	Imparting information	Group continuing education Nutrition group for clients Sex education group for adolescents Sensory-motor group for preschoolers Reality orientation group for nursing home residents
Supportive/ Therapeutic	Dealing with emotional stress	Group for infertile spouses Group for expectant spouses Group for middle-aged people in midcareer crisis Group for people with chronic illness processes Group for rape victims

care planning? What is the most effective way for the nursing service to function? How can nursing personnel best provide nursing care for a group of 25 patients? How can the nursing staff deal more constructively with Mr. A's behavior? How can members of this community be assisted to improve their level of wellness? How can nurses take political action?

Task groups are usually under pressure to complete the task within an allotted time period. There is also a tendency to ignore, deny, or try to smooth over any existing conflict.

Teaching Groups

The primary purpose of *teaching groups* is to impart information to the participants. Although the tendency to separate the learner from the teacher always exists in these groups, at least one research study has shown that students learn as much—or more—when teaching as their peers do (Clark, 1976).

Nurses may participate in a number of teaching/learning groups. Hospitals, institutions, and agencies often present continuing education courses to teach nurses new skills or to enhance previously learned basic skills; in many of these programs, nurses participate with a group of other nurses. A nurse may, on the other hand, utilize the group format in a program designed to teach clients about health care.

When the nurse leads a group in which the primary purpose is to teach or to learn, the following questions need to be considered: Which material is best suited to group or individual learning? Are the students ready to learn? What do they already know? Do the members of the group have similar levels of knowledge? How much repetition of material is needed to enhance learning? How can students be helped to plan and evaluate their own learning experiences? Is the pace of instruction too fast or too slow? How can the teacher provide the students with adequate feedback about how well they are learning the material? How can effective learning behaviors be increased?

Innumerable subjects are suitable for handling via the group-teaching format: labor and childbirth techniques; birth control methods; nutrition; the management of diabetes; the management of colostomies or ileostomies; effective parenting; orientation to nursing home living; appropriate exercises for nursing home residents; sensorimotor skills for preschoolers; preparation of families to enable them to care for discharged family members.

Supportive or Therapeutic Groups

The primary purpose of *supportive or therapeutic groups* is to assist members in dealing with emotional stresses due to hospitalization, illness processes, growth and development crises, situational crises, or socially maladaptive behavior. Supportive or therapeutic groups focus on the examination of members' thoughts, feelings, and subsequent behavior. Clients often benefit from ventilating their feelings, from seeing that others share and accept these feelings, and from learning healthy and constructive ways of coping with them. Supportive or therapeutic groups should not be thought of as a form of group psychotherapy or of psychoanalysis; rather, their concern is to prevent possible future upsets by educating the participants in effective ways of dealing with emotional stress arising from situational or developmental crises.

Supportive or therapeutic groups are usually under less pressure than the teaching and task groups to complete the task during one or two meetings. Another difference is that conflict among the group members may be pursued and explored because it is often related to the ways in which members deal with emotional stress. The leader may even choose to maintain anxiety and conflict at fairly high levels if this serves to assist the group to continue focusing on their feelings, rather than to cover over or withdraw from the discomfort. New tasks, such as how to deal with the entrance of a tardy or new group member, may be generated spontaneously and dealt with by the group.

In convening a supportive or therapeutic group, the nurse frequently gathers together people who are undergoing similar emotional stresses. Such groups may, for example, consist of families of the dying; individuals with a chronic illness and/or their families; individuals who have recently lost a body part through surgery or accident; the severely burned; individuals awaiting diagnosis, admission, surgery or hospital discharge; involuntary nursing home residents; rape victims; parents of infants with birth defects; clients with a drug or alcohol problem; prison inmates; those with suicidal or homicidal tendencies; middle-aged men or women facing a career or midcareer crisis; anxious preschoolers who fear going to school; child-abusing parents; adolescents with inadequate knowledge of their current physiological changes and the ramifications; and identified or potential juvenile delinquents.

CONCERNS OF ALL GROUP LEADERS

Although at first glance it would seem that each group would demand different group skills, actually, to be effective, *all three types of groups require that a balance be maintained between adhering to the task and meeting the interpersonal needs of group members.* For example, if task group leaders are so concerned about following the agenda that they fail to note how upset the curriculum committee is about a proposed cut in faculty salaries, the group will not function effectively. Likewise, if leaders in teaching groups are so concerned about giving information that they forget to find out whether all members understand the information, or if they support dependency on the leader by always giving the correct answer themselves, group functioning will not be as effective as it should be. Even in supportive or therapeutic groups, leaders have to maintain a balance between giving support and working toward a task; since the task may be to understand one's thoughts and feelings and to learn effective ways of dealing with them, leaders cannot be too supportive as this may prevent group members from learning new ways of coping with their thoughts and feelings. Thus, in all three types of groups, nurse leaders are concerned with achieving a balance between interpersonal and task functions, and with system difficulties. Some questions to ask in this regard are:

- What patterns of behavior are developing in the group?
- Which patterns promote positive growth and which seem to promote negative growth?

• What can be done to promote primarily positive growth?
• How can subsystems be influenced to have congruent interests with the larger group system?
• What can be done to enhance openness in the group system?
• What is contributing to closedness in the group?
• What common group patterns and what unique group characteristics does this group have?

QUALITIES OF AN EFFECTIVE GROUP LEADER

Group leaders must have a high tolerance for anxiety, frustration, and disorganization. They must be capable of accepting group confrontation, hostility, and conflict without directly or indirectly punishing group members or ignoring the fact that such processes are occurring.

A group leader needs to be able to accept and organize a great deal of information and be capable of observing both verbal and nonverbal messages and making sense out of both. Group interactions can be intense and quick-moving, and the amount of input can overwhelm the novice group leader. With practice and supervision by a skilled group leader, nurses can learn how to organize extensive amounts of information and when and how to intervene in group interaction. At times, the nurse leader must be able to stop listening to what is being said in the group and instead "tune in" on the nonverbal communication that is being conveyed.

Group leaders have to engage in a certain amount of preparation for each session. This includes becoming informed about the task at hand and thinking of ways of structuring the meeting to delegate some responsibility to group members and to enlist their aid before and between meetings. Effective teaching requires that the teacher digest the information about the topic to be taught and plan how to present it to the learners "in their language" and on cue. Further, effective teachers are able to establish a give-

and-take rapport with learners and to provide feedback and support in order to help group members to feel comfortable when talking, practicing, or demonstrating in the group. A supportive or therapeutic group leader has to reread logs or recordings of past sessions, look for evidence of nonparticipation by members who may need attention or for strong feelings or opinions that need exploration in future sessions, and be alert for patterns of interaction that seem to be developing. Supportive or therapeutic group leaders are quite likely not to have an agenda or teaching plan in mind, but are aware of potential problem areas and move to intervene when appropriate. They must be willing and able to seek out assistance in understanding group processes; knowing when supervision from a more experienced group leader is needed is a very important quality to have.

A sense of humor is also a great asset to a group leader. Despite adequate preparation for group sessions, unforeseen circumstances can disrupt the best-laid plans. Being able to detect the humor in unexpected situations allows the group leader to ride with the ebb and flow of group processes without becoming irritated, angry, punitive, or withdrawn. Such a leader can often use humor as a way of decreasing group tension levels.

In theory, nurses promote independent action in clients but, in practice, nurses "do for" patients in many instances and are comfortable in the role of authority or expert. In a group setting, the nurse who can promote independence and more effective behavior and encourage group members to be more responsible for what takes place in the group will be the more effective group leader. However, in the beginning limits need to be set on who will be part of the group, where the group will meet, and what topics will be discussed. The leader will also need to decide how group members will be prepared to enter the group. These somewhat competing goals of fostering independence yet structuring the group require a blend of skill that can be acquired through practice in group leadership and through the study of group processes.

Another asset of effective group leaders is the ability to blend their own style of relating to constructive communication techniques. Some leaders may believe that asking, "What's with Betty and Tom?" seems too informal, even rude. Others may think that saying, "It seems the group has some feeling about what John said," sounds stilted or too formal. Group leaders develop their own choice of words and their own ways of conveying the same idea. Learning to apply communication principles in a clear, direct manner takes quite a bit of practice.

Group leaders' willingness to examine their own expectations for the group and to deal with them realistically is an important aspect of group leadership. They may deny wanting the group to proceed in a certain way, yet feel quite frustrated when it does not proceed as expected. For example, the nurse leader of a health discussion group may have in mind that 10 preplanned health topics will be covered in 10 weeks. If the group members have many questions, cannot absorb the information, or are concerned about other issues, the group will probably not proceed as the leader expected, who is then likely to react with anxiety, frustration, anger, and resentment. Effective group leadership requires that nurses examine their own expectations and acquire the ability to correct or change them if they turn out to be unrealistic. This may evoke further anxiety in nurse leaders, but it is a necessary side effect of learning. Decisions about how or when to intervene with a group are based on group needs and system patterns, not the nurse leader's need for security, self-esteem, or support.

Being appointed a group leader does not mean that the respect and influence of the title necessarily follow. Acquiring a leadership title such as head nurse, supervisor, assistant director of nursing or director of nursing brings with it unexpected disappointments and uninvited problems. The nurse leader must be prepared to encounter suspicion, distrust, hostility, subservience, passive resistance, insecurity, jealousy and resentment.

Nurses who went to lunch with the newly appointed group leader may now avoid, exclude, act defensively, become more guarded in their conversations, may make more critical comments, or "apple polish." Stubborn resistance and negativism to new plans or helpful suggestions may emerge.

Becoming a group leader invariably brings about significant changes in relationships with group members. Negative reactions to those in power and authority are part of everyone's behavior—even the group leader's. Children develop ways of coping with authority figures, including crying, getting sick, becoming compliant, withdrawing, buttering up, forming alliances, lying, hiding feelings, bullying or dominating, striking back, ridiculing, resisting, defying, aggression, perfectionism, blaming others or tattling, and cheating (Gordon, 1977, p. 15).

Identifying one's own and group members' reactions to authority figures is the first step in becoming an effective group leader. Using the unique dynamic interplay between leader and group members without taking member reactions personally will assist the group leader to help the group move forward effectively.

NURSING DIAGNOSIS

Table 1-2 presents *nursing diagnoses* that may be especially pertinent to group work with clients.

EFFECTIVE AND INEFFECTIVE GROUPS

According to Johnson and Johnson (1975), an *effective group* is one that accomplishes its task(s), meets interpersonal needs, and develops and grows in effectiveness. Effective groups are even capable of changing goals and matching individual needs to group goals. The nurse leader is aware of how effective groups work and strives to promote behaviors that lead to effective functioning. In order

**TABLE 1-2 Nursing Diagnoses Pertinent to
Group Work with Clients (Carpenita, 1984)**

Diagnosis
Diversional activity deficit
Thought processes, alterations in
Anxiety
Fear
Self-concept, disturbance in
Communication, impaired verbal
Grieving
Parenting, alterations in
Social interactions, impaired
Social isolation
Violence, potential for
Coping, ineffective individual

to accomplish their task, all group members must be aware of exactly what this task is.

In ineffective groups the goals are unclear, the group remains uninvolved or uninterested, and the given tasks often seem to promote competition rather than cooperation and collaboration.

In effective groups, communication between the leader and the group members and among the group members themselves is open, direct, and clear. Accurate expression of thoughts and feelings is encouraged. Individuality is supported, while activities that foster a closer working relationship and enhance the "common good" are encouraged. In such groups a high level of trust, support, safety, creativity, and constructive controversy is evident.

In ineffective groups, communication is usually a one-way affair, from the leader to the group. Ideas are expressed, while feelings are denied or ignored. No attempt is made to involve group members in group functions. The emphasis is on conformity, and the leader seems most interested in the control of the group, in making sure that there is order and stability, and in maintaining the status quo.

Power and leadership are shared by all members in effective groups. The leader teaches the group members how to be effective, and members participate in decisions according to their ability. Controversy and conflict are assessed as possible clues to involvement and interest in the task. Members learn how to recognize problems and how to solve them with a minimum of energy and a maximum of satisfaction; they also learn how to evaluate the effectiveness of their solutions and, finally, the effectiveness of their group.

Leadership in ineffective groups is often based on seniority or authority. Participation of members is unequal; authoritarian members dominate the group and make decisions. Controversy and conflict are ignored, avoided, or squelched. Group members do not learn how to solve problems or how to evaluate their effectiveness as group members or as a group. The status quo is maintained.

In summary, the group leader promotes effective functioning by:

• Clarifying the group task
• Changing the group task to match individual and group goals (when necessary)
• Promoting collaboration and cooperation
• Promoting security, trust, support, and creativity
• Encouraging constructive controversy
• Teaching group members to share leadership and responsibility in the group
• Teaching group members to problem solve and to evaluate group functioning and resultant outcomes

WAYS OF LEARNING ABOUT GROUP FUNCTION

Learning to be an effective group leader cannot be accomplished merely by reading about group concepts and processes. An effective group leader has to have not only the theoretical knowledge about how groups work, but also the ability to assess group concepts and processes and to intervene in real-life groups. Assessing and intervening in group processes requires practice supervised by an experienced leader.

One way to learn about group functioning is to join a task, teaching, supportive, or therapeutic group. As participants, nurses can observe and study group concepts and processes in action. They might also study group processes more effectively by becoming observer/reporters for the group. In this role they focus their energies on listening and recording and not participating verbally in the group interaction.

Prior to intervening in real-life group situations, nurses can practice interacting in simulated situations; these have many learning advantages that real-life situations do not have. First, simulations contain less risk than real-life situations; learners know they are only "pretending." Less risk in simulations can often lead to less anxiety about an unknown situation, and to more potential for learning. Second, simulations allow learners to receive feedback for group behavior and skills; they can observe the consequences of their behavior without being so concerned about disclosing their feelings, receiving disapproval from authority figures, or psychologically "damaging" clients. Third, since group simulations are structured to contain elements of possible real-life group situations, experience in simulation is likely to increase nurses' ability to handle real situations more easily. Fourth, simulations are a "fun" way to learn, and motivation is usually high. By practicing some or all of the group simulations found at the ends of the first six chapters of this book, nurses who are preparing to become group leaders can achieve all four of these benefits.

The next step in learning to be an effective group leader is actual practice in assessing and intervening in group process. This can occur through taking the role of designated group leader either in a new group or in an already established group of clients, families, or health personnel. Being designated leader requires the output of more energy and the assumption of more responsibility, at least initially, than does assuming a group member role, a recorder role, or an observer role. Ultimately, the designated leader in an effective group shares responsibility and teaches group members how to assume responsibility for group decisions. Nurses can also practice being group leaders by taking the informal leader role in a group; once they are aware of how and when to intervene, they can assume formal leadership functions in a group.

SIMULATED EXERCISES

Each of the three simulated exercises that follow includes an experiential and a discussion component. When using Exercises 2 and 3, large groups should be divided into subgroups of not more than 15 members. Following the simulation, the entire group reconvenes for the discussion.

Ample space should be provided for subgroups to spread out, and chairs should be movable. When subgroups are too close there is a tendency to listen to others' discussions.

EXERCISE 1   Perceived Problems of Being in a Group

Objectives
1. To provide practice as leader, recorder, and listener in groups.
2. To compare and contrast the listening and telling skills of various participants.
3. To examine common concerns regarding being in group situations.

Procedure
1. The group or the instructor appoints a timekeeper.
2. The group or the instructor appoints a leader who directs the exercise.
3. The leader says, "Arrange yourselves into subgroups of three. One will be the recorder who writes down what is said, one will be the listener, and one will be the speaker who tells what problems one faces in group situations." (Variation: have the speaker tell what problems are anticipated as group leader.)
4. When the small subgroups are arranged, the leader asks the timekeeper to call time when 15 minutes are up. The leader gives the signal to begin.
5. When the timekeeper calls time, the groups scramble, so that each person plays a different role for the next 15 minutes.
6. When the timekeeper calls time, the entire group convenes for a group discussion.
7. The group may appoint a leader to focus the discussion.
8. The leader asks the timekeeper to remind the group when only 10 minutes remain for discussion. Generally, 25 to 50 minutes is an adequate length of time to cover the issues, but the amount of time required will increase with an increase in the size of the group.
9. The following issues can be used as topics for discussion:
   a. What did the recorders in each group observe?
   b. What helpful or not helpful attitudes did the speakers in each group perceive in their listeners, i.e., nonverbal clues of attention, support, boredom, etc.?
   c. What did the listeners observe about the speakers?
   d. How does a listener encourage a speaker to speak?
   e. What skills are required by a recorder as compared to a speaker or listener?
   f. Did the recorder interfere with speaking and/or listening; if so, in what way?
   g. What concerns were expressed about being in (or leading) a group? (These may be written on a chalkboard or shown in overhead projection transparencies and used for reference purposes.)
   h. How could each concern be handled in the most effective way? (Refer to Chapters 1–3 and 5 for specific interventions.)
   i. How can what was learned in this exercise be applied in actual group situations?

EXERCISE 2 Introductions

This exercise is designed to give the nurse leader practical experience in giving, hearing, and analyzing group introductions without the risks that would be involved in actual patient or staff group situations.

Objectives
1. To practice introducing self to others.
2. To observe how others present themselves to the group.
3. To observe group processes characteristic of the orientation phase of groups.

Procedure
1. The group or instructor appoints a timekeeper. The timekeeper makes sure that each person's introduction does not exceed 3 minutes. Whenever a group member takes more than 3 minutes, the timekeeper turns to the next member and says, "Next, please."
2. The group or the instructor appoints a leader for each group.
3. The group leader appoints a recorder from among his group members. The recorder is asked to jot down observations regarding how people introduce themselves, how group members react toward being asked to introduce themselves, and the level of and changes in group cohesiveness.
4. The group leader asks the group members, "Will each of you introduce yourself to the group, say what you do, who you are as a person, and why you are participating in this exercise? Who will start?"
5. When all group members, including the leader, have introduced themselves, the entire group convenes.
6. A discussion leader volunteers or is appointed by the group. This leader asks the recorder to assist by helping the group to present their observations concerning the following issues:
   a. Did people tend to use socially acceptable, rational introductions? If so, is this characteristic of the orientation phase of a group? If not, what explanations does the group have for the presence or lack of more openness?
   b. Do nurses seem more likely to stereotype themselves than others might? Why?
   c. Why do people seem hesitant and cautious about expressing themselves in the group? If some people gave too much personal information, what might be an explanation for that type of behavior?
   d. Did group members really seem to get acquainted during the introductions? Why, or why not?
   e. What information seems most helpful for the leader to give during her introduction?
   f. What information seems most helpful for group members to give other group members during introductions?
   g. How can what was learned in this exercise be applied to actual group situations?

Variation: Two leaders can work together to lead the discussion. In this case, the following discussion question can be added:
   h. What advantages and disadvantages were there to coleadership? (Refer to Chapter 6.)

EXERCISE 3 Paraphrasing

This exercise provides practice in listening to and restating what others say. Many times the receiver of a message makes judgments about what the other has said and responds to these judgments rather than to the other's message. Because effective leadership requires expert listening and restating skills, this exercise can be redone whenever the group leader begins to notice a tendency toward interpreting group members' messages without sufficient basis for the interpretation.

Procedure

1. The group or the instructor appoints a timekeeper, who is to make sure that time limits set for each step are kept; the timekeeper also is to remind the group at appropriate intervals how much time remains.
2. The group decides on time limits for each step.
3. The group or the instructor appoints a leader for each group.
4. Each member is asked to talk about the best thing that happened this week. One member starts by telling the person to the right in the group the best thing that happened. The second person paraphrases what the first person has said, using different words to describe what happened without adding new information. The exercise continues in this manner, with one person recounting the best thing that happened, and the next person paraphrasing, followed by another person telling about a best experience and another person paraphrasing that experience until everyone has either told or paraphrased. (Variation: Use a highly controversial topic.)

15–30 minutes
5. The leader then asks group members to reverse roles and have the person who told of the experience become the paraphraser.

15–30 minutes
6. The entire group discusses the following points:
   a. What is difficult about paraphrasing another person's statements?
   b. Who in the group found it easier to tell a story than to paraphrase a story? Who found the reverse to be true? What ideas does the group have about why this might occur?
   c. What do the "speakers" have to tell the "paraphrasers" that may help them be more effective reflectors of what was said?
   d. What was learned from this exercise that can be applied in real-life group situations?
   e. (Optional) What effect did the controversial subject have on the ability to paraphrase?

READINGS

Brandt, M. A., et al. (1985). Follow the leader: A learning exercise . . . Select a leader/manager to interview and observe at work. *Journal of Nursing Education* 24(4),139–142.

Carpenito, L. (1984). *Handbook of nursing diagnoses.* Philadelphia: J. B. Lippincott.

Clark, Carolyn C. A. (1976). Comparison of learning outcomes for teacher and student players in a peer-mediated, simulation game for associate degree nursing students. *Fourteenth Annual NASAGA Conference Proceedings.* Los Angeles: University of Southern California Press.

Gordon, T. (1977). *Leader effectiveness training.* Wyden Books.

Johnson, D. & Johnson, F. (1975). *Joining together: Group theory and group skills.* Englewood Cliffs, NJ: Prentice-Hall.

Laird, M. (1975). Techniques for Teaching Pre- and Postoperative Patients. *American Journal of Nursing* 75,1338–1340.

Mezannotte, E. (1970). Group instruction in preparation for surgery. *American Journal of Nursing* 70,89–91.

Ramshorn, M. (1970). The Group as a Therapeutic Tool. *Perspectives in Psychiatric Care* 8,104–105.

Rosini, L. A., et al. (1974). Group meetings in a pediatric intensive care unit, *Pediatrics* 53,371–374.

Salzer, J. (1975). Classes to improve diabetic self-care. *American Journal of Nursing* 75,1324–1326.

Smith, E. D. (1971). Group Conferences for Postpartum Patients. *American Journal of Nursing* 71,112–113.

Tappan, R. (1983). *Nursing leadership concepts and practice.* Philadelphia: F. A. Davis.

Wittes, G. & Radin, N. (1971). Two approaches to group work with parents in a compensatory pre-school program. *Social Work 16,* 42–50.

2
Basic Group Concepts and Process

GROUP CONTENT AND PROCESS

Content, or *group content,* are terms used to describe topics discussed in a group session. Content may be straightforward and explicit, or it may convey a symbolic meaning. Both explicit and symbolic meanings are assessed when one group member comments, "Boy, is it hot in here!" at a time when other group members are arguing with one another. Overtly, the room may be warm temperature-wise; symbolically, the group member may be commenting on the "hot" issue being discussed. With practice, an experienced leader can tune into both straightforward and symbolic meanings being expressed in the group.

In groups there is constant movement toward and away from the goal as group members seek to reduce the tension that arises when people attempt to have their individual needs met, yet engage in group tasks or interactions. This movement is referred to as *group process.* Group process refers to the *way* group members interact with one another: interruptions, silences, judgments, glares, scapegoating, and more are all group processes. Because so much activity occurs in some groups, the inexperienced leader often has difficulty identifying group process. In the group process approach the leader assumes that the group is not only an aggregate of individuals, but a dynamic, ever-changing ebb and flow of energy. When tension levels are too high or too low, group process is impeded. For each group the leader must be able to identify what group processes are occurring, what will impede and what will assist group process, when to intervene in the process, and when to remain silent.

The following excerpt from an adolescent health discussion group points up the leader's lack of awareness of group process and shows how he impedes effective group movement:

LEADER: "You guys shouldn't drink, you know."

TONY: "What do you know about it?"

LEADER: "Drinking is bad for your health."

TONY: "That's what everyone says."

LEADER: "So why not listen?"

TONY (burps loudly): "Pass the beer, please."

SAM: "Enough talk for today."

LEADER: "O.K., since you don't want to talk, we'll end for today."

Here, the leader seems to be at war with the group and tries to use logic to convince the members that drinking is unhealthy. Had the leader realized that the members of this group would be likely to resist logical arguments (which they would probably have heard before from authority figures), he might have taken a different tack, such as asking them what drinking did for them, what they knew about the physiological effects of alcohol, or even whether they thought that he would tell them what everyone else had told them. In this way, the leader might have decreased group resistance to his statements and possibly begun to convince the group that he was interested in listening to them and understanding their perceptions. By taking such a role, he would not only potentially reduce group tension, but also serve as a role model for effective group interaction. The leader also assumes the group does not want to talk, when only one member indicated there had been enough talk (Sam). Querying the other group members would have been a useful intervention. Also, the leader makes a unilateral decision to end the group. It would have been helpful to either (a) stick to the limits of time the group had agreed on, or (b) get a group consensus on whether or not to end.

As group leaders continue to observe group process over time, they will find it useful to ask a few questions:

- What seems to lead to increased tension levels?
- What indicates conflict?
- When does the group seem to be apathetic?
- How are decisions arrived at?
- What types of leadership occur?
- What rules for behavior are in operation?
- What factors lead to effective movement toward and away from group goals?
- What signs of aggression and assertiveness are evident?
- What phase of group process does the group seem to be in?
- What themes recur?

Process comments focus on the here and now of what is happening. Some general process comments are: "I wonder what is really going on in the group now." "Why are we doing this?" and "I believe we are getting bogged down by feelings right now." More specific process comments depend on what is occurring, but some possibilities are: "Were you all aware that only two people voiced their opinions, yet we made a decision?" "Did you know that Jim and Betty have formed their own discussion group?" and "I think we're really all very confused and angry by what just happened; let's discuss it."

This chapter will describe key group concepts and the dynamics of group process.

TENSION AND ANXIETY IN THE GROUP

At times, all group members, including the leader, show signs of tension or anxiety. Mild and even moderate anxiety can be useful in promoting group movement. When the tension level becomes too high, the leader takes steps to lower it, after noting which indicants of anxiety increase and which decrease, and at what points during the session this happens.

Anxiety is an unexplained feeling of discomfort that one experiences when expectations are not met. New group members may experience anxiety when they expect the group experience to be of one sort, and it turns out to be something else. Group members can also experience anxiety when asked questions about any topic on which they lack information or feel unsure of themselves. For example, a group member who is obese may experience anxiety when diet is discussed, and a group leader who does not have correct information on a certain drug may feel anxious when asked to discuss that drug. Anxiety is a common reaction in unfamiliar or new situations; the first meeting of a group may result in such feelings in both group members and the leader. Some people are quite sensitive to disapproval and may feel anxious when the leader or other group members indicate disapproval of their words or actions. Any situation that interferes with basic needs can create anxiety. Not being respected or recognized can lead to feelings of anxiety; leaders who are challenged by group members or group members who are called by inappropriate or incorrect names may experience anxiety.

Anxiety can occur whenever human needs are threatened. *Maslow's hierarchy of needs* provides a framework for assessing group members' anxiety. The lowest level of human needs is physiological in nature. A group member who complains of being tired or hungry is exhibiting Level 1 human needs. When group members are afraid of censure or feel insecure in their jobs or statements,

Level 2 human needs for safety are threatened. When group members are talking and joking with one another, they may be attempting to meet their need for acceptance (Level 3). Group members who seek approval of their work or press to get the group moving to accomplish the work may be working on Level 4 needs for esteem. Group members who evolve creative solutions to problems may be working toward Level 5 needs for self-development and self-actualization (Maslow, 1970).

Many groups and organizations do not provide sufficient opportunities for their members to satisfy Level 4 and 5 needs. When leaders exercise arbitrary power, group members may be unable to move past Level 2 because their needs for security and safety are constantly being threatened. Group members who are not provided with sufficient opportunity to meet higher level needs will seek opportunities off the job. This may explain work situations in which workers slack off and only use enough energy to keep their jobs and receive their pay.

Signs of anxiety include restlessness, lack of eye contact, body tenseness, stiff or repetitive gestures, rapid shallow breathing, perspiration, rapid or unclear speech, changing the topic of conversation, silence, distorting or overreacting to others' comments, griping, daydreaming, or being forgetful.

Group leaders can follow several procedures to reduce anxiety in new group members. First, spending time with the members prior to the first group session will help them feel more comfortable, because they will then know at least one person who will be in the group. Also, leaders can share with group members the reasons why they are leading the group and what their feelings are at that moment. Admission of their own feelings of tension or anxiety about starting a new group will often help the members to feel more comfortable in sharing their own thoughts and feelings. Leaders can anticipate that in an unknown situation group members will be curious about what role will occur. Inviting comments from the group about what they expect of the leader and stating specifically the functions the leader plans to perform can decrease tension.

Warming-up exercises may be quite helpful in decreasing anxiety in a new group. One exercise consists of having members write down and/or verbally explain the reason they are there and what they hope to get from the group experience. Or, to get the group started, the members can be asked to draw pictures of themselves and then pair off to talk about their drawings and possibly to express their fears about being in the group. Films and other audiovisual materials can be used to stimulate discussion. The innovative leader can devise many such warming-up exercises.

When group members are unable to talk about their discomfort, yet the leader senses that tension is high, one of the following comments can be made: "It seems we're all a little tense," or "I guess we're all a little nervous since we don't know each other yet," or "I sense this subject worries you," or "This is hard to learn, but it will be worth the effort."

Group leaders can prepare themselves and group members for meeting anxiety-provoking situations as they arise. One way to do this is to think through, or even write down, a summary of what one expects to happen in the coming session. This technique will help identify hidden fears, and once this is accomplished further self-questioning can include such queries as: "So what if that does happen?" "What could I do to handle that if it did occur?"

Role-playing can also be used to decrease anxiety. Suppose a group member becomes anxious when asking for a raise, when setting a limit on a child's behavior, or when asking for a favor. Two group members, or the leader and one group member, can preplay the problematic situation; then the two role players can exchange roles to find out how it feels to "be in the other's shoes." Group members can serve as coaches to the role players and give feedback after the role play about how the situation could best have been handled.

Progressive relaxation can be used to reduce group anxiety at the beginning, middle, or end of a group session or meeting. Group members can be asked to close their eyes, get comfortable in their chairs, and concentrate on the leader's voice. The following words can then be said in a slow, monotone voice:

Each time you exhale, let your breathing move lower in your body, moving effortlessly toward your abdominal area. (Pause.) Focus your attention on your feet now; let your feet sink into the floor, becoming more relaxed and comfortable. (Pause.) Let that feeling of relaxation and comfort move up your feet into your lower legs. (Pause.) Continue to let your breathing move effortlessly toward your abdominal area, so that each time you exhale, your breathing becomes easier and more relaxed. (Pause.) Continue to let that feeling of relaxation and comfort move up your legs. You might want to picture the relaxation moving up your body as a color or symbol; use whatever is right for you. (Pause.) Let the feeling of relaxation and comfort move up your legs and into your buttocks; let your buttocks and groin relax and sink into the chair. (Pause.) Let your lower back and spine sink comfortably into your chair; let all the muscles in your back relax and get longer and wider. (Pause.) Let anything you're carrying on your shoulders roll down your shoulders, down your arms, and out your fingertips. (Pause.) Let your neck relax and float between your shoulders and head. (Pause.) Let that feeling of comfort and relaxation move up your scalp and hair, over the top of your head, and down your forehead; let your eyebrows relax. Let your eyelashes and eyes relax and the space behind them and the space behind that. Release all unwanted thoughts from your mind, getting more relaxed and more comfortable. Let your cheeks relax. (Pause.) Let your nose relax. (Pause.) Let your mouth relax; unlock your jaw and let it relax. (Pause.) Let your teeth and tongue relax. (Pause.) Scan your body and find any areas that need more relaxation; send some peaceful relaxation there. (Pause.) When you're ready, slowly open your eyes, keeping the sense of relaxation and comfort with you.

Imagery can also be used to assist group members to relax. Ask the group to close their eyes and take a trip to a relaxing, comforting place. It can be a place they have been before or someplace they have never been. Encourage the group to smell the smells associated with the peaceful and relaxing place; hear the sounds associated with the peaceful and relaxing place; taste the tastes and experience the sensations associated with the peaceful and relaxing place. Be silent for 2 to 3 minutes as the group totally emerse themselves in the peaceful and relaxing place. After several minutes, ask the participants to come back through time and space to the group, keeping the relaxation and comfort with them. Remind group members that they can become more relaxed and comfortable at any time by closing their eyes and returning briefly to their peaceful and relaxing place.

In addition to anxiety in the early stages of a group, there may be upsetting situations that occur. At these times, group leaders can use either of the relaxation exercises described above to assist group members to relax and to communicate better with others in a calm and thoughtful manner.

These relaxation exercises can also be used to decrease anxiety about upcoming situations. The first step is consciously to contract and then relax the various body muscles. This allows the learner to "get the feel of" tension and relaxation. Next, he imagines a pleasant scene. When he is completely relaxed, the anxiety-provoking situation is called to his attention, and, as soon as he feels his body becoming tense, he is asked to focus again on relaxing his muscles and imagining the pleasant scene. With practice, the learner will be able to go through an entire tension-provoking scene mentally without experiencing overwhelming anxiety. Once he has mastered relaxation in role-playing situations, he can practice the exercise in actual anxiety-provoking experiences (Fensterheim, 1971).

Group leaders can reduce group members' anxiety by assisting them to meet low-level human needs and by allowing them to share in creative problem solving.

Finally, humor can be used to dissipate tension. However, it should be used cautiously so that group members are not made to feel degraded, and it should never be used to avoid confronting important issues.

GROUP CONFLICT

Conflict caused by opposing forces within the group can occur in an individual member, or it can be shared by subgroups or by the entire group. An individual can experience conflict within himself when he wishes to be singled out for special treatment by the leader yet at the same time fears the leader's disapproval; this conflict can be resolved when the individual conforms to the behavior of the other group members. Another solution to bids for special attention by one group member is for the group to take over and interfere with the attention-getting behavior.

Sources of conflict in the group as a whole include being given an impossible task, having conflicting loyalties within and outside the group, jockeying for power or status, dislike of one another, and involvement in the task assigned. Whether the group leader should intervene in a group conflict depends on whether group process seems to be impeded or assisted by it. Intervention may be necessary when some group members attack others' ideas before they are completely expressed, take sides and refuse to compromise, attack one another's personal attributes or behavior, insist that the group does not have the knowledge or experience to resolve their difficulties, or accuse one another of not understanding. Whenever any of these symptoms of conflict occur, the leader may intervene by stating the group goal more clearly, defining smaller steps that can be taken to assure obtaining the goal, suggesting that more time be allowed to achieve the goal, teaching the group what they need to know to reach their goal, finding a goal that interests all members, requiring members to substitute an assertive statement such as, "I feel angry when people tease me" for an aggressive, attacking, "You teased me, you rat!" and asking group members to paraphrase others' comments in order to decrease distortion of communication messages.

When group members appear not to understand the group goal, frequently disagree, and show strong positive or negative feeling and signs of impatience, the group leader will probably not want to interfere, since these are signs of conflict arising from involvement in the task.

Conflict is best viewed by leaders as a challenge and an inevitable part of human interaction. Conflict is not likely to surface until members begin to feel relatively comfortable with one another; prior to that, they are more concerned about what others may think of them. As politeness fades in importance, squabbles or subsystem grouping may occur as human differences and disagreements are noticed and addressed. Group leaders can assist their groups to learn to deal with conflict by:

- Teaching and encouraging the use of assertiveness and feedback skills
- Increasing openness
- Reinforcing and commenting on *any* positive group action
- Testing for *true* consensus
- Identifying hidden agendas
- Facilitating win-win solutions
- Changing seating arrangement
- Using negotiation skills

Teaching Assertiveness and Feedback Skills

The language of conflict can elicit feelings of threat or defensiveness; group members can close off from one another. The language of assertiveness is one of problem solving that elicits trust and positive regard for openness and directness. Parts of group members unknown to themselves can be opened and released for constructive work when feedback is given. Novice group members may refrain from giving feedback because they are fearful of hurting or angering the recipient. Constructive feedback will minimize hurt and anger and open the person to discovery of information which was previously unknown.

Many nonconstructive group patterns can be successfully

resolved if all group members practice assertive communication. Learning to take responsibility for one's own thoughts, feelings, and actions takes the attack out of confrontation. Group members will be more likely to remain nondefensive when assertive comments such as, "*I* feel angry about what is happening," or "*I* want to give you feedback about your nonverbal messages Sarah," are made than when aggressive comments are: "I feel *you* are manipulative," or "You're always disrupting the group by groaning." By teaching group members to take the blame out of their comments, refrain from unfair fighting by bringing up past issues, to focus on observed behaviors, and to clearly state the issues, group leaders can teach communication skills useful not only in the group at hand but in many other interpersonal situations as well.

Group leaders can make a pact with the group that the leader or any group member can interrupt the conversation whenever a nonassertive message is heard. This will assist all group members to be aware of nonassertiveness. At these times, the person who used a nonassertive message can be asked to "Say that again, only this time use an 'I' message." With repetition, group members will begin catching their own nonassertive messages midway through their statement and correcting themselves.

One method for describing the language of problem solving was developed by Eric Berne (1964) and Thomas Harris (1969). Their method of describing communication processes is called, *Transactional Analysis* (TA). A *transaction* occurs when one person says something to another and the second person responds verbally or nonverbally.

Transactions are categorized by Berne as *The Parent, The Adult,* and *The Child.* Parent and Child developed unconsciously or without much control by the individual. The Child is composed of recorded memories of feelings and fantasies; rage, sadness, or fear occur when the Child portion takes over. The Parent is composed of recorded memories or messages remembered from parental speeches; messages concern how to eat, dress, behave acceptably, what one "should" and "should not" do, what is good and what is bad. The Parent is the judgmental part of oneself.

Although TA has been called simplistic, it does provide an easily teachable framework for group communication. The idea is Adult to Adult communication in which problem solving occurs through getting and giving descriptive (rather than judgmental) information.

When a group member says, "You are frightening" a Parent statement and a judgment has been made; when a group member says, "I feel frightened when you look menacing," an Adult statement has been made. By teaching group members to identify Parent, Child, and Adult messages, problem solving will be enhanced; much of what bogs down problem-solving processes is the occurrence of judgmental and helpless statements.

Problem solving is facilitated when all group members have the same information. Preparation for problem solving requires establishing an openness among group members. Just as individual group members can learn to deal at the adult level of transaction, individuals can learn to give feedback in a manner which minimizes judgment, fear, threat, and defensiveness. Some rules to teach group members to use are:

1. *Be descriptive rather than judgmental.* For example, when a nursing supervisor tells her supervisees, "You're not providing quality care," they are likely to be pained or angry. If the nursing supervisor tells her supervisees, "I noticed Mr. Smith's light has been on continually, let's talk about how to help him rest comfortably," then the staff can focus on a specific problem and will be more receptive.

2. *Be specific rather than general.* Saying, "I don't like your attitude," gives far less help to the person than "I get the impression I'm not being listened to."

3. *Give feedback when it can be used.* Check with the recipient to find out whether the individual wants the feedback and can use it at that time. If a group member is anxious or depressed, feedback can add more stress to a stressful situation. Ask the group member when feedback

can be given or check back later that session or at the next meeting to agree on a time for feedback.

4. *Give feedback at the time the behavior occurs.* If a nurse leader says to a staff member, "I observed you talking with Mr. Jones last week and I didn't like what I heard," the details of the incident are likely to have been forgotten.

5. *Give feedback when its accuracy can be checked with others.* The group is the best place to give group members feedback. Avoid waiting until after a group meeting to have a private chat with a group member.

6. *Use assertive "I" messages when conveying criticism or feeling.* Saying, "Don't argue with the physicians, you'll get me in trouble " is far more threatening than, "I feel uncomfortable when I hear you argue with Dr. Gonzales, let's do some role-playing so you can discuss and not argue with him."

McKay, Davis, and Fanning (1983) describe *rules of fair fighting* that can be used by group leaders to teach group members how to discuss disagreements, grievances, and gripes:

1. *Hit above the belt.* Group members must learn to become attuned to criticism that is too painful for other group members to hear and that which can be heard, accepted, and acted upon. The best way to identify what is too painful is to validate with the group member whether a subject is too painful to be discussed at that moment and to respect the individual's decision. Topics that require discussion are not avoided, merely put on hold until the group member is ready to discuss them; group leaders are generally responsible for picking up the topic at a later time.

2. *Practice good timing.* Avoid storing grievances and attacking them all at once, or bringing up a "hot" topic just as the group is about to end.

3. *Be clear.* State the grievance simply using "I" statements that make it clear that "this is my feeling, not your fault."

4. *Focus on behavior, not attitudes.* Demanding respect, warmth, or any subjective, spontaneous attitude is doomed to failure. Doomed comments ("I feel you don't respect my opinions and I want you to") can be turned into successful conflict resolution statements by focusing on behavior. ("I feel left out of important decisions that affect me; I want to go shopping with you and pick out the gift.")

5. *Focus on the here and now.* Leave past disagreements or hurts out of the discussion. Fight about one specific issue at a time.

6. *Focus on one individual at a time.* Avoid raging at group members who are absent at the time or at other groups, institutions, religions, ideas, etc.

7. *Listen attentively* to the other person's gripes and avoid rehearsing a retort, hearing only what you want to hear, blowing up or walking away, anticipating what the other person means or will say next, or judging what is said.

Increasing Openness

Sometimes conflict can be decreased by increasing openness. Some strategies for increasing openness are self-disclosure, nonverbal and verbal mirroring, using open-ended questions, and checking out perceptions.

When the group leader discloses feelings and opinions, group members often feel more comfortable doing so themselves. Group leaders must walk the fine line between burdening the group with personal problems and showing humanness. A useful rule is to think through whether the self-disclosure is being used to make the group leader feel better or whether it is being used to facilitate group movement.

Nonverbal and verbal mirroring can reduce conflict. In one group, the leader purposefully changed her breathing pattern, gestures and eye movements to mirror the behavior of a hostile group member; later in the session, that group member became less verbal and mentioned feeling closer to the leader.

Hover (1983) discusses using *Neuro-Linguistic Programming* methods to enhance communication in the family group. Neurolinguistic programmers have noted that individuals have a primary representational system for their inner experience. Those using a visual representational system use words such as see, observe, my point of view, my perception, and my focus. Those using an auditory representational system use words such as I hear, I like loud sounds, I enjoy soft noises, and I harmonize well with others. Those using a kinesthetic representational system use words such as I feel, I sense, I touch, I'm aware of. . . . Those using an olfactory-gustatory representational system use words such as I can almost smell . . . , I enjoy the flavor of . . . , I taste, and I eat . . .

Group leaders can open communication with group members by "speaking their language."

The following example shows what happens when the group leader *does not* speak the group members' language:

LEADER: "How are you *feeling?*"

GROUP MEMBER: "It *looks* like the day may brighten."

LEADER: "But tell me your feelings."

GROUP MEMBER: "I just did!"

The next example shows what happens when the group leader identifies and uses the same representational system as the group member:

LEADER: "How are you feeling?"

GROUP MEMBER: "It *looks* like the day may brighten."

LEADER: "So that's how things *look* to you today."

GROUP MEMBER: "Yes, you're right."

Merely by matching the verbal predicates, the leader and group member were able to communicate at a higher level of understanding. Many group members describe the experience of verbal and nonverbal mirroring by saying, "All of a sudden we were on the same wavelength. I felt more understood."

Using open-ended questions can encourage group members to describe and understand conflict. The following are open-ended questions:

"What are we arguing about now?"
"What do you think is preventing us from moving along?"
"What is your opinion?"

When the leader or any group member *assumes* what is meant by another person, conflict and negative feelings can result. To ensure conflict is not the result of assumption, it is wise to check out perceptions with questions such as, "I hear you saying. . . . Is that what you mean to convey?" "If I hear you correctly, you're saying . . ."

Reinforcing Positive Group Action

Group members may become discouraged as they struggle to become a working, constructive system. Group leaders can reinforce and encourage group action by pointing out *any* progress toward the goal. Some comments exemplifying this are: "I realize you are feeling frustrated with making this decision, but we are showing progress by discussing alternatives." and "Conflict is a normal happening in groups; I think we should congratulate ourselves on our courage in attempting to resolve it!"

Testing for True Consensus

It is not unusual for group leaders to take a cursory hand count to settle an issue. Group members may feel pressured to respond as the majority does, despite feelings to the contrary; this can result in resentment, lowered self-esteem, and conflict. Group leaders can assist the group toward true consensus by using the following behaviors:

1. Refrain from calling for a vote until all group members have had their say.
2. Continuing to ask, "Who else has a comment?" or repeating, "We haven't heard everyone's ideas yet," until all have spoken.
3. Restating that all members' viewpoints are needed in order to attain a true consensus.

Identifying Hidden Agendas

Hidden agendas are operating goals that influence group process even though they are not openly acknowledged. McKay, Davis, and Fanning (1983, pp. 77–84) list eight major hidden agendas that disrupt clear, open communication:

1. *I'm Good.* The theme of how honest, hard working, courageous, loyal, generous, successful, powerful, or self-sacrificing one is may be used by group members who have this hidden agenda. Group leaders can be helpful to group members using this agenda as a life tune by assisting them to accept the position: "I'm a mixture of strengths and weaknesses."

2. *I'm Good, But You're Not.* Group members who use this agenda may be heard to say, "Everyone's stupid, incompetent, selfish, unreasonable, lazy, frightened, or insensitive but me." Eric Berne (1964) has identified versions of this agenda, including (a) *Courtroom* (spouses try to prove how awful the other is; in groups, group members can make statements discounting other group members' involvement or contribution to group goals), (b) *If It Weren't For You* (spouses or group members blame each other for restricted, joyless lives or sessions). A healthier position to teach group members is: "I'm no longer in the business of comparing."

3. *You're Good, But I'm Not.* A simple version of this agenda is flattery; more complex forms involve worship of

smart, beautiful, or strong people. This agenda is often used to ward off rejection or anger or as an excuse for not changing. Group leaders can teach group members to accept the position: "I don't need to make excuses; I can get attention with my strengths and abilities."

4. *I'm Helpless, I Suffer.* This is the agenda of the victim who refuses to be responsible for what happens to himself or herself. *Ain't It Awful* is a variation played by those who want to complain about their spouses. Group leaders can identify the game, *Why Don't You. . . . Yes, But,* when they hear group members constantly asking for advice and help and then not taking it. This version is very good for maintaining helplessness. Teaching group members to say, "My life is a balance of pleasure and pain, hope and sadness," can give them a less helpless view of their lives.

5. *I'm Blameless* is used by group members who use excuses for their failures. *See What You Made Me Do* is used by group members who ask for suggestions or advice, follow the advice, and then blame the group leader or group member who suggested it.

6. *I'm Fragile* is used by group members who present themselves as vulnerable, in need of protection, and unable to hear the truth from others. Group members choosing the I'm Fragile agenda can learn to accept "It scares me a little when someone is honest, but I can listen to it."

7. *I'm Tough* is the agenda of group members who list all the harrowing things they do daily and still survive. The message is they are stronger; work harder, faster, and longer than anyone else. I'm Tough is also the message of the dangerous and violent who are saying, "don't attack me or I'll hurt you." I'm Tough hides the vulnerability and fear of rejection inside. A healthier message to learn is: "I can take care of myself while relaxing and without scaring others."

8. *I Know It All* is the agenda of the teacher/lecturer. Moralizing, constant teaching, or preaching keeps others away from intimacy and protects one from the shame of not knowing and not being adequate. A healthier message is: "I can learn from others by listening and watching."

Group members can learn to identify their own agendas by counting the number of times they use an agenda, verbalizing the fact that an agenda is used. ("I know I'm sounding helpless, but it's not so" or "I'm sounding down on everyone and everything, but I know it's not that bad.")

Group leaders can share information on the basic eight agendas and point out instances of use during group conversation. (e.g., "We seem to be playing, *Why don't you. . . . Yes, but*" or "I'm hearing a hidden agenda, does anyone else hear it?") Group members can be encouraged to write down their new life positions on three-by-five cards and carry them with them, complete a sign to hang in their room, or say them over and over as affirmations or mottos.

Facilitating Win–Win Solutions

Win–win solutions are focused on ends or goals. In win–lose and lose–lose methods of conflict resolution, the following commonalities can be identified (Filley, 1975, p. 25):

1. There is a clear we–they distinction between group members or groups rather than a we-versus-the-problem.
2. Energy is focused on total victory or total defeat.
3. Each sees the issue from its own point of view, not in terms of mutual needs.
4. Emphasis is on attaining a solution, rather than upon defining goals, values, or motives to be attained with the solution.
5. Conflicts are personalized rather than depersonalized via an objective focus on facts and issues.
6. There is no planned sequence of conflict-resolving activities nor a differentiation of them from other group processes.
7. The parties are conflict-oriented, emphasizing the immediate disagreement, rather than relationship-oriented, emphasizing long term effects of differences and how to resolve them.

To facilitate win–win solutions, group leaders can suggest that participants (1) focus on defeating the problem, not each other; (2) avoid voting, trading, or averaging; (3) seek facts to resolve dilemmas; (4) view conflict as helpful; (5) avoid self-oriented behavior and focus on others' needs or positions; (6) seek solutions which are not unacceptable to anyone (i.e., either falls in the category of "don't care" or "support"); and (7) agree that the leader controls the process by which the group arrives at agreement but does not dictate the content.

Research on problem solving (Lawrence and Lorsch, 1967) has demonstrated that confrontation (win–win solutions) leads to higher performance in organizations than either force (resorting to authority or coercion) or smoothing (agreeing on an intellectual level). Whenever possible, the group leader should attempt to teach group members conflict-resolution skills that lead to win–win solutions.

Sometimes conflict occurs because of subsystem formation or *pairing*. Prior to intervening, it is wise to observe if the seating arrangement may be contributing to subsystem formation; if this is the case, the leader can separate group members who seem to be splintering off from the group. Depending on the maturity of the members and the type of group, several methods can be used to achieve the same purpose.

In a supportive or therapeutic group, the leader can "call process" and say to the group, "It seems we're not all talking together; what do you think that is about?" Through discussion, the group may identify the problem; if not, the leader can suggest a seating change or another method of assisting group members to talk to the entire group.

Sitting in a circle is the most conducive to discussion. If a task or teaching group is not arranged in a circle, arranging chairs in that manner can promote discussion. Asking all group members to sit next to someone different is a tactic useful for breaking up subgroupings. If the group leader introduces chair changes in a neutral manner the group is likely to comply (e.g., "Let's try sitting in different chairs today; this will give you a different perspective on what happens and also may be a positive factor in promoting discussion").

The group leader can also arrange to sit between group members who are pairing or subgrouping; this will break up the subgroup. Sometimes subgrouping is due to feeling alienated from or competitive with the leader; by sitting next to the subgroup members, the leader will seem less formidable and less competitive.

By sitting next to an anxious, hostile, or new group member, the leader also signals a wish to be closer and more supportive. The author has found this useful in therapeutic and supportive groups, especially when other group members signal nonverbally that they are fearful of the group member. The physical presence of the designated leader can provide a calming influence on the group and also signals that the group leader is not fearful or rejecting of the group member.

The following situation describes a successful solution to subgrouping:

A group of nursing students in a BSN completion program taking group leadership was composed of seven students who did not know one another and two who worked in the same health care facility. The two who knew one another previously always sat together, whispered when others were talking, and talked about one another to the group. When the leader noticed the pattern, she suggested everyone take a seat next to someone different at the next session. At the end of the class, the leader asked what effect the change of seating arrangement made. A number of group members stated they were surprised how different the group seemed; one group member said, "It's because Barbara and Jennie weren't sitting together!" Jennie commented, "When I made my presentation it was easier because I didn't feel I had to speak only to Barbara." The leader then used the incident to discuss the pros and cons of changing seating arrangements in the groups the group members were currently leading.

Using Negotiation Skills

Anytime the leader or group members want something from each other, a potential negotiable situation exists.

Negotiation skills assist individuals in getting what they want from others without alienating them. *Negotiation* is a process through which people with different or even opposing needs arrive at a fair agreement by generating a mutually acceptable option.

Mckay, Davis, and Fanning (1983, pp. 147–148) say the process can be broken down into four stages:

1. *Preparation.* Before meeting with those involved, each person decides what outcome is desired and what would be less satisfactory but still acceptable. During this phase gathering of information to bolster your case, strategic planning, and brainstorming occur. During *brainstorming,* all possible ideas are written down, avoiding judging the merit of each; one idea often sets off another idea, and judging merit interferes with the process. Once all possible ideas are compiled, they are ranked in order of usability.

2. *Discussion.* During this stage, each person asks for the other's interests and elaborates on their own point of view. Each person describes the facts of the situation and their thoughts and feelings about the situation. Discussion is the major means of resolving deadlocks.

3. *Proposal/Counterproposal.* One person makes an offer or request, the other(s) make counteroffers. This cycle is repeated until a compromise is reached; there may be timeouts for a return to Stages 1 and 2.

4. *Agreement/Disagreement.* Disagreement is a natural step in negotiation; it signals the need to try again by returning to earlier stages. Eventually a mutually acceptable option will be reached.

The following example describes how one group negotiated with its leader:

Preparation: One of the group members was going to be absent for the next meeting and asked that the session be tape-recorded. The leader asked the group to decide, but gave information on the pros and cons of taping the session, such as it will help the absent group member to stay on track with the movement of the group, the tape can be saved and used by the group to study its own behavior, taping the group may inhibit some group members from speaking (at least initially), procedures for ensuring the group session is taped and confidentiality is preserved must be developed. The leader then asked the group to brainstorm about how to deal with the group members' request.

Discussion: The group members asked why the person would be absent and elaborated on why it was important to be at each session. Feelings of hurt, resentment, and envy surfaced.

Proposal/Counterproposal: The group member who was to be absent proposed that she leave her tape recorder and several tapes with the group leader and asked for a volunteer to be responsible for taping the session and meeting her the following day to deliver the tapes. Several group members remained unsure about being taped and suggested a group member call the absent member during the week to fill her in on what had happened. One group member pointed out that much of the detail of the session may be forgotten and one group member's perception of the group session may be inaccurate.

Discussion: The group continued to discuss the merits of recording and not recording.

Agreement: The group finally agreed to allow the session to be taped under the condition that the group member guard the tape from others' ears and return the tape to the group at the following session. The group would have access to the information on the tape for that session, and then the tape would be erased.

The following rules for principled negotiation can be used by group leaders:

1. Keep position separate from self-worth, so that an attack on a position is not perceived as a personal attack.

2. Avoid entering negotiations with a single, rock-solid position. Instead, begin negotiations with a comment such as, "We're here to discuss how we can. . . . When you hear our requests, we think you'll agree they are reasonable and will probably want to make some suggestions of your own."

3. Use active listening to elicit others' feelings, thoughts, and needs. "The way I understand it is that you're *afraid* someone might hear what you said. You *think* the informa-

tion might be used against you. You *need* to feel secure and nonthreatened here."

4. Share feelings, thoughts, and needs honestly. "I have mixed *feelings* about being here next week without Dorothy here too. I think *taping* is a good idea because we can use the tape to learn more about how we are doing. It will provide another source of feedback." "I would *need* a volunteer to be responsible for the safe use of the tape to agree to the idea."

5. Uncover the interests behind an opponents' position; be sensitive to basic human needs for security, trust, intimacy, and self-esteem (Maslow, 1970).

6. Help others save face by labeling compromise as generosity. (e.g., "I appreciate your generous offer to compromise on this issue.")

7. Explore trade-offs such as time for money, flexible hours for money, free overtime for future salary increase, etc.

8. Turn options into proposals by using "yesables": a yesable proposal is an acceptable option stated as a direct question to which "yes" is an easy answer. The following are deniable proposals: "I want this report and I want it by 10 o'clock!" and "No matter what you say you're assigned to Mr. Jones." Turning the proposals into yesable proposals would mean saying, "Would you rather finish the report now or give it to me after lunch?" or "If I assign you to Mr. Amos today, will you work with Mr. Jones tomorrow?" If you have trouble getting a "yes" from the person, check to be sure that that person has the power to make the requested decision.

Negotiating with an Opponent Who Has All the Power (Bosses and So Forth)

When faced with an opponent who has all the power, odds are tipped toward losing unless the other person(s) "plays fair." If the best alternative is a strong, realistic one, the proposal can be stated as an ultimatum: "If I don't get this promotion, I plan to leave institutional nursing and start my own private practice." If leaving is not possible, the best alternative is to come down hard on objective criteria: "What is it I'm doing that is keeping me from getting this promotion?" Appeal to an opponent's sense of fair play; drum up support among like-minded people; form a committee to study salary increases; or hold meetings, rallies, and press conferences. Become an expert on what other hospitals are paying and shine the harsh light of publicity on an opponent's unfairness.

Negotiating with Hard-liners Who Will Not Cooperate

When management refuses to consider a position, look behind their position for underlying interests. Make a list of all the reasons they might have for refusing. When prepared, make an appointment with management and ask, "Why do you refuse to consider my proposal?" Sit back and wait out the silence for an answer. If you get a non-answer like, "It's against hospital policy " ask, "Why is it against hospital policy?" Also, try more specific questions: "Is it too expensive?" "How expensive do you think it would be to implement my proposal?" "Are you afraid others will try to take advantage of you if you give in to me?"

When management comes on strong with personal attacks, redefine them as attacks on the problem. For example, if accused of stirring up trouble, stifle impulses to call the boss a stooge for stupid management; instead, reframe the attack by saying, "You're right, nurses are very stirred up about staffing, and I appreciate the fact that you feel strongly about it too. It's a serious problem that deserves the attention of all responsible leaders at this hospital." By reframing attacks as shared problems, hostility can be defused and hardliners have a graceful way to start cooperating.

If there is too much feeling on both sides, the "one-text" procedure has been known to work. A text of a possible agreement is drawn up and presented to both sides; if both turn it down, another text is drafted and another, until an agreement is reached. The success of this method is due to the lack of direct confrontation or argument in the face of extremely high feeling states.

Negotiating with Opponents Who Play Dirty

There are many dirty negotiating tactics including lies, deceptions, bribery, blackmail, and psychological warfare. The best way to handle opponents who use these tactics is to "call process"; that is, stop talking about the subject at hand and talk about the process that is occurring. (e.g., "Before we go on, I'm having trouble concentrating on what you're saying because you're shaking your finger in my face. Let's move to the sofa instead of sitting across from each other at this desk.") If necessary, indicate an understanding of the temptation to take every possible advantage and that such attempts are not taken personally. Invite your opponent to help look for options that benefit everyone. Suggest some objective criteria for judging the agreed-upon options.

When this approach does not work, call in a neutral mediator. There are some conflicts that just cannot be negotiated. These occur when one or more individuals want the conflict more than the resolution. For example, unions may want to keep feelings high until a contract deadline closes; management may want to prolong negotiations until the union's funds are exhausted; students may want to prolong grading reform to keep high visibility through publicity. Hidden agendas must be uncovered before conflict can be negotiated in these cases (McKay, Davis, & Fanning, 1983, pp. 147–158).

GROUP APATHY

When group members show indifference to the task, appear bored, and seem unable to mobilize their energies or to persevere, they may be using *apathy* to deal with high anxiety. An apathetic response is a withdrawal reaction; it can be used as a disguise for tension and discomfort.

Group leaders need to intervene whenever the following signs of apathy are noted: tardiness, absenteeism, attempts to end meetings early, minimal participation by group members, frequent yawns, dragging conversation, loss of the point of a discussion, reluctance to assume responsibility for group functioning, precipitous decisions, failure to carry through on decisions, or lack of preparation for coming meetings.

Leaders need to determine the source of apathy before intervening. Group members can be asked such questions as:

- What do you think about the group goal?
- Is the group goal relevant to you?
- What meaning does the goal have for you?
- What do you think will happen if you attain the goal?
- Do you think the group atmosphere lends itself to sharing and cooperation?
- Do you have the skills you need to communicate easily with one another?
- Is effort toward achieving the group goal clearly organized and coordinated?
- Have you been asked to make decisions you think will not be acted upon?
- Do you think I make unilateral decisions?
- Does conflict between a few members overshadow group movement toward the goal?

Once the source of apathy has been identified, the leader can act to overcome it. If the task goal was imposed by others or by the leader, the group can be helped to decide on a goal that the members consider more relevant. If group members fear punishment, the leader can help the group to explore whether this fear is realistic; if it is, perhaps the leader's expectations need to be reexamined. If group atmosphere is too tense, or if the room is crowded, noisy, poorly ventilated, or otherwise not conducive to effective group interaction, action can be taken to modify the milieu. If the group lacks communication skills, these can be taught through the use of the simulated group exercises at the ends of the chapters of this book and by role modeling effective communication behavior. If efforts toward achievement of the group goal are not clearly organized or coordinated, the leader may wish to rethink approaches and/or seek supervision from a more experienced group leader. If decision making leads to meaningless or unilateral decisions, the leader needs to teach the group more effective ways of arriving at meaningful decisions. If conflict overshadows group movement toward its goal, the leader must determine the sources of the conflict and intervene appropriately.

NORMS AND COHESIVENESS

Norms are rules for behavior within the group. Each member will bring to the group his own ideas about appropriate behavior with others. If group members are drawn from highly divergent social, economic, educational, or cultural groups, it may take quite a while for them to agree on appropriate group behavior.

Despite the attitudes the individual members contribute, certain norms will be developed spontaneously within the group. Because norms refer to expected behavior, they carry a "should" or "ought to" quality, and some beliefs may be carryovers from childhood experiences. The leader may set a rule for behavior, but the group will accept it only when the behavior it calls for is rewarded and enforced by other group members.

Group leaders can use several techniques in establishing norms. They can look for the presence of already existing norms and for norms that seem to be developing. Norms can be initiated by leaders who may suggest, "I think we should share our thoughts and feelings now." They can have an even stronger influence on group norms by demonstrating, through their own behavior, what appropriate group behavior is. Instead of merely suggesting that others share their thoughts and feelings, the group leaders might share their own. This would allow others to see that it is safe to express themselves and would also serve as a model for expressing oneself in the group context. Leaders share feelings when it seems to be helpful to group process and refrain from doing so when the expression would simply serve to meet the leader's needs for attention, sympathy, or retaliation.

Norms can work in favor of or against group cohesion. *Cohesiveness* is the attraction of the group members for each other. Highly cohesive groups are motivated to work effectively toward group goals and to satisfy all members' interpersonal needs. The more favorable the expectations are that members have about group membership, the more attractive will the idea of group membership be. The leader can influence attraction to the group by making sure that everyone has the same goals in mind, that group goals are relevant and clearly stated, that paths to goal attainment are known and rewarded, and that cooperation among members is promoted.

Some *measures of cohesiveness* are arrival on time, full attendance at group meetings, a high trust and support level within the group, the ability of the group to tolerate individuality and have fun, the ability to work cooperatively with other group members to enforce agreed-upon norms, and ease in making statements of liking for the group or for group members.

Groups cannot become highly cohesive unless all members, including the leader, interact on an equal basis. The leader can increase cohesiveness by helping group members to feel part of and equal within the group, by controlling group functioning effectively, and by teaching members how to give and get satisfaction or affection from working with each other. The leader tries to include all group members in the discussions by asking for everyone's opinion and

by seeing withdrawn or silent members individually between meetings to discover their reasons for nonparticipation. The more frequently group members interact with
each other, the more likely it is that the group will become
cohesive. To promote group interaction, leaders may deflect
some of the questions from themselves to a group member.
Frequency of group meetings can also affect cohesiveness,
since the more frequently a group meets, the higher the
potential for interaction; the leader may consider increasing the frequency of the meetings if other attempts to promote cohesiveness fail. Another way to influence cohesiveness is to help the group to identify similarities that exist
between members; this technique increases a sense of community in group members.

Group cohesiveness is strongly influenced by the balance
between members' needs to control others in the group.
This need ranges from wanting to control all aspects of
everyone else's behavior to abdicating control entirely because the situation is unsafe or unhealthy. When leadership is shared by all group members, all will learn to control some aspects of group functioning and to accept control
in others. Leaders demonstrate appropriate control levels
by structuring the group, yet allowing it to assume responsibility for some decisions.

Leaders can increase affection among group members
and feelings of satisfaction or pride in accomplishment by
planning meetings so that the potential for success is high.
To do this, they do not place group members "on the spot"
by requiring them to answer after they have stated that
they do not feel like talking at that time, and do not allow
others to do so. Group members are rewarded for cooperation and goal attainment by receiving comments on goals
reached and not by receiving comments on poor performance except, perhaps, to suggest additional ways of
attaining the goal.

Allowing group members to express hostility and conflict
will also increase cohesiveness. Unless anger or resentment
are openly expressed, they will go underground and impede

member cooperation and interaction. The group leader conveys the idea, directly and indirectly, that it is "O.K. to talk about anger and differences here."

THEMES

Although many topics may be discussed by a given group or even in one group session, one predominant *theme* can usually be identified. At first, it may seem that group meetings are disconnected and that the subjects discussed or the activities pursued are unrelated. Yet a pervading theme can often be identified. It may not necessarily be logical or overt; it may be implied through association, symbolic meaning, or feeling tone. For example, one group of nursing home residents kept returning to the topic of exploitation of nursing home patients for the financial benefit of the government, and how change was needed; all the group members became animatedly involved in the discussion whenever this topic came up. On one level, a discussion of this kind could be taken at its surface value; on another level, the leader in this instance became aware that nursing home residents felt exploited and used by society and even perhaps by the nursing home staff.

The feeling of being exploited, mistreated, and used is a common theme in group sessions in long-term institutions such as psychiatric hospitals and prisons. The feeling of being different occurs as a theme in group sessions when all members have the same illness or handicap. Prenatal discussion groups may have themes of fear of pain and of the birth experience. Groups composed of people who are all at a particular stage of growth and development may exhibit themes characteristic of that period; for example, 4- to 6-year-olds in a group may have a theme of competition, while an 8- to 11-year-old group may have a theme of industry.

Not every group will have one of these common themes. The group leader needs to be attuned to the possible linkages and underlying consistent meaning of what is expressed in group interaction that may imply a theme or ongoing group concern.

SIMULATED EXERCISES

Each of the two simulated exercises that follow includes an experiential and a discussion section. If the group is large, it should be divided into subgroups of not more than 15 members. Following the simulation, the entire group reconvenes for a discussion period. If an exercise is completed without an instructor or supervisor present, participants should plan to share difficulties and insights with an experienced group leader following completion of the exercise.

EXERCISE 1   Sharing with Others

This exercise gives learners the opportunity to practice sharing information about themselves in a nonthreatening environment and to learn to listen to other group members who also share information about themselves. It also provides an opportunity for learners to observe how sharing can influence group cohesiveness.

Objectives
1. To develop skill in sharing information about self with others.
2. To develop a recognition of safe levels of self-disclosure.
3. To learn to listen to what others wish to say without prodding or debating.
4. To enhance group cohesiveness.

Procedure

1. The group decides the time limits for each section of the exercise.
2. The group or the instructor appoints a timekeeper, who makes sure that time limits for each section are observed. The timekeeper also reminds the group at appropriate intervals how much time remains.
3. The group or the instructor appoints a leader for each subgroup.

10 minutes per person maximum

4. The subgroup leaders ask group members to write down three questions they would like to be asked by others. Questions should deal with interests, hobbies, family, friends, beliefs, hopes, goals in life, or activities. All members write down three questions, sign their name, and pass the paper to the subgroup leader, who asks members to answer their own three questions. The leader makes sure that personal information is shared and discussed on a voluntary basis. Whenever group members feel like going on to another question, they are free to do so. There is to be no argument or debate. All are free to state their position without argument from others.

15–30 minutes

5. When all group members have been asked their three questions, the subgroup leader asks each group member to tell one new thing learned about every other group member.

15–30 minutes

6. The entire group then meets to discuss the following points:
   a. What was easy and what was difficult about this exercise?

(continued)

EXERCISE 1 (*continued*)

---

    b. How did this exercise affect how group members feel about one another?

    c. How did group members decide how much to tell others about themselves and how much to withhold?

    d. What prevented group members from listening actively to one another?

    e. What was learned from this exercise that can be applied in other group situations?

EXERCISE 2 Giving and Receiving Help and Feedback

This exercise requires two individuals to help a third solve an interpersonal problem through taking on the roles of consultant and observer.

Objectives
1. To gain skills in defining a problem and helping another person solve a problem.
2. To practice feedback skills.
3. To identify Parent, Adult, and Child statements and the effect of each on communication.

Procedure

	1.	Divide the group into subgroups of three people.
5–10 minutes	2.	Distribute materials so that each subgroup has one copy of: Presenter Instructions, Consultant Instructions, and Observer Instructions (see pp. 56–57).
	3.	Each group decides who will play which role.
	4.	Each member reads his or her instructions.
15 minutes	5.	The Presenter presents his or her problem to the Consultant. The Observer remains silent during the presentation.
5–10 minutes	6.	The Observer gives feedback to both Presenter and Consultant, including behavior that helped or hindered the consultation process.
25 minutes	7.	Group members trade roles and proceed with Steps 5 and 6 above.
25 minutes	8.	Group members trade roles and proceed with Steps 5 and 6 above. (At the end of this round, each person should have played all three roles.)
15–45 minutes	9.	All group members assemble and discuss the following: a. Which role was easiest for you to play? Give ideas why this is so. b. What feedback skills do you need to polish? c. What presenter skills do you need to hone? d. What do you need to practice more to be a more astute observer? e. What problems did consultants encounter? f. What problems did presenters encounter? g. What problems did observers encounter? h. How can these problems be overcome?

(continued)

EXERCISE 2 (*continued*)

Presenter Instructions
1. Your task is to consider a problem which you are presently experiencing. Make sure it is a problem you feel strongly about and one you need help with.
2. Take a few moments now to think about some specific problem you are directly involved with. Make sure it is a problem that: is unresolved, that you are ready to do something about, that involves you and at least one other person, and that is very important to you.
3. Once you have selected the problem:
   a. Describe the problem in detail, specifying what the problem is, who is involved, and the specifics of what is involved. When describing the problem to the consultant be sure to describe the facts (your thoughts, feelings, and actions and what was said or done by others). Do not judge or comment on what you did or plan to do.
   b. Describe the factors or situations that led up to the problem, and why you think the problem persists.
   c. Describe how you could solve the problem. Describe things you could do and any difficulties you think might arise if you try to implement your solution.
   d. Describe how solving the problem might affect you and the other(s) involved.
4. When you are ready, signal the others and prepare to describe your problem using 3a, 3b, and 3c above.

Consultant Instructions
1. Your task is to help the presenter define or redefine the problem and the relationships involved in *specific* terms so that steps toward solving the problem can occur.
2. Some questions you may want to ask the presenter are:
   a. "How do you see yourself in this situation in terms of personal responsibility for what occurs?"
   b. "What is the fundamental difficulty in the situation?"
   c. "Who does or says what in the situation to create a problem?" (You may want to break this down into specifics: "What was said first?" "What was said next?" etc.)
   d. "What does not occur that could help resolve the problem?"
   e. "What seems to prevent it from occurring?"
   f. "What solutions have been tried?"
   g. "How have the things you tried worked?"
   h. "What do you plan to try for your next solution?"
   i. "In what way can I be of help to you?"

3. When discussing the problem with the presenter:
   a. Avoid taking over the problem by saying, "You should . . ." "The real problem seems to be . . ." Instead, ask the presenter, "How do you see what is happening?" If you see things entirely differently, say, "I wonder if it could be that . . ." (and then let the person know your perspective).
   b. Avoid minimizing the problem. Resist making comments such as, "We had that problem, and it was easy to solve," or "That's not such a problem, you can solve it."
   c. Ask questions beginning with what, where, how, and who.
   d. Help the presenter focus on what he or she can do, not on what others in the situation can do.

Observer Instructions
1. Your task is to watch and listen to the presenter and consultant very carefully. Remain silent. Take notes so you will remember exact words said, gestures, and postures.
2. While observing ask yourself:
   a. What is going on between the consultant and presenter? Are they warring; not listening to each other; trying to convince, judge, talk down, or understand? Write down anything said or done to support your conclusion.
   b. What does the consultant do to help the presenter speak freely?
   c. What does the consultant avoid doing that could help the Presenter speak freely?
   d. Does the presenter stay with defining the problem before trying to solve it?
   e. Does the consultant stay with defining the problem before trying to solve it?
   f. What specific examples can I provide of the presenter using parent, adult, or child language or behavior?
   g. What specific examples can I provide of the consultant using parent, adult, or child language or behavior?
3. Use the rules for feedback when making your report to consultant and presenter. (You may wish to write down your feedback comments for later use or you may want to make copies of your feedback comments and give them to each person.)

READINGS

Beeber, L. et al. (1986). Cohesiveness in groups: A concept in search of a definition. *Advances in Nursing Science, 8*(2), 1–11.

Berghan, P. (1985). The use of assertiveness training in the clinical environment. *Journal of Nursing Education, 24*(1), 33–35.

Berne, E. (1964). *Games people play.* New York: Grove Press.

Bradford, L., Stock, D., Horwitz, M. (1953). How to diagnose group problems. *Adult Leadership, 12,* 12–19.

Fensterheim, H. (1971). *Help without psychoanalysis.* New York: Stein and Day.

Filley, A. (1975). *Interpersonal conflict resolution.* Glenview: Scott, Foresman, and Co.

Harris, T. (1969). *I'm OK, you're OK: A practical guide to transactional analysis.* New York: Harper and Row.

Hover, D. (1983). Enhancing family communication using neurolinguistic programming. In I. Clements and F. Roberts (Eds.), *Family health: A theoretical approach to nursing care* (pp. 83–92). New York: Wiley.

Lawrence, P., Lorsch, J. (1967). *Organization and environment, managing differentiation, and integration.* Unpublished master's thesis, Division of Research, Graduate School of Business Administration, Harvard University.

Maslow, A. (1970). *Motivation and personality* (2nd ed.). New York: Harper and Row.

McKay, M., Davis, M., Fanning, P. (1983). *Messages: The communication book.* Oakland, CA: New Harbinger Publications.

Trunzo, T. (1985). Group conflict—A challenge to participative management. *Hospital Topics, 63*(1), 36–39.

Watzlawick, P., Weakland, J., & Fisch, R. (1974). *Change: principles of problem formation and problem resolution.* New York: Norton.

3
Working to Achieve Group Goals

PHASES OF GROUP MOVEMENT

The phases of group movement may be classified according to several systems. Perhaps the simplest system divides the group into three phases: orientation, working, and termination. During the *orientation phase,* group members are seeking to be accepted in the group and to find out how they are similar to and different from the other members. Their expectations for outcomes of group experiences are often unrealistic. For example, it is highly unlikely that long-term behaviors will be changed by four to six sessions of a supportive group. And certainly expecting to be cured of cancer in a supportive group is totally unrealistic. Anxiety is high during this phase, and there are frequent bids for the leader to perform unreasonable feats and to be all things to all group members. The leader may have to be quite verbal in the first few meetings in order to teach group members how to relate to one another and how to move toward the group goal. As the group proceeds, members may directly or indirectly express anger toward the leader for not being able to meet all their needs. It is important that the leader stick to realistic goals, while at the same time assisting group members to express their thoughts and feelings regarding what happens in the group.

Given time and appropriate leadership, groups will evolve in mature or working stage groups. Groups may proceed from the orientation stage to the working stage without completely finishing the tasks of the former; in this case, the group may need to go back at a later date to complete them. Some groups end before arriving at the working or mature group stage.

Uncertainty and insecurity are characteristic of groups in the orientation phase. Group leaders should be aware that they also may experience these feelings during this phase; awareness may help leaders move through the stage focusing on assisting the group to achieve the tasks of the phase without hurrying the group to relieve leader anxiety and discomfort.

In the orientation phase, group members are polite and formal with one another. Safe topics are discussed. Members maneuver to keep others at a safe distance and prevent confrontation, retaliation, and rejection. As the orientation phase proceeds, nurse leaders can assist the group to move to the working phase by being a positive role model and engaging in more open communication than other group members. Other group members will follow once they see it is safe to be more open. Referring to the group by name, for example, "our staff group," will help group members identify with the group. Referring to group behavior as "*we* are . . ." "*we* seem to be . . ." will also help group members begin to think of themselves as an entity.

In the orientation phase, group leaders may have to summarize group sessions and ask what topics group members want to discuss the next time. A signal that the group is moving into working phase is that group members summarize and volunteer ideas for upcoming meetings. Group leaders who are too rigid or too unstructured during this phase may prevent the group from feeling support, having a clear purpose, and being guided to complete individual and group goals. The two examples that follow demonstrate ineffective and effective leader behavior.

Example 1: Ineffective Leader Behavior
A cutback in funds at City Hospital upset many staff members. The staff met with the head nurse to express their concern and to demand action be taken to obtain needed funds for nursing care supplies.

The head nurse spent most of the meeting reading a memo from the director of nursing. The head nurse was worried that the staff would blame her for what had happened and she was apprehensive during the meeting. When the memo had been read, the head nurse spent time trying to explain to the staff why the funds had been cut back. When the head nurse finally finished, the staff took turns asking questions about why the cutback had occurred and how it would be handled. They gradually realized that the new administrator was cutting back funds from all services. One staff nurse suggested a meeting with the administrator. No more time for discussion was available and the meeting broke up at that point.

The head nurse was more concerned about her feelings than group functioning. She controlled the flow of group interaction too rigidly, allowing insufficient time for discussion and problem solving.

Example 2: Effective Leader Behavior
The head nurse on unit C was told by the director of nursing that within 2 years all units would be converted to primary nursing. Each head nurse was to prepare her staff and tell LPNs that they would no longer be eligible to work on the unit. The head nurse felt anxious about meeting with her staff, but prepared by learning relaxation techniques and using role-playing to practice responses to anticipated staff hostility with two supportive head nurses from other units. The head nurse's two peers gave her helpful feedback on her defensive nonverbal behavior.

When the head nurse met with her staff, she gave a very short introduction about implementing primary nursing and then asked for their reactions. After some expressions of anxiety, hostility, and insecurity, the group settled down to discuss the meaning of this decision to each of them. The group decided to explore alternative ways of upgrading the education of the LPNs, bring in other LPNs from hospitals where primary nursing had been implemented, and set short-term goals for implementing the long-term goal of primary nursing.

The head nurse was aware of her feelings of anxiety and insecurity, but she took constructive steps to deal with them. By opening up discussion to allow expression of feelings, this group was able to move to problem solving.

By assisting group members to use assertive, confrontive communication, group leaders can assist groups in moving away from the angry, tension-filled stage of the orientation phase. Group leaders can ask that group members discuss their feelings rather than act them out by walking out of the group or hollering at one another.

During the *working phase,* when the group has learned to work together cooperatively, the leader needs to intervene less frequently. Leadership functions are shared. Positive and negative feelings may be expressed, control issues are worked out to the satisfaction of all, cohesiveness increases, norms are solidified and reinforced, and progress is made toward attaining the group goal.

Nurse leaders teach group members how to provide needed leadership functions in the working phase. When feasible, instructions for various group leadership roles can be given to group members and they can provide the needed functions (see Simulated Exercises for group role assignments).

As the group enters the working phase, decisions are more apt to be made by consensus than by vote. Problem solving is common. Frustration and discouragement about the group is replaced with cautious optimism. Group members turn less often to the leader for help. Nurse leaders function most effectively in this stage by helping the group from getting sidetracked, encouraging problem solving and consensus decision making. There is less need to reinforce ground rules or provide support for group members. A measure of group maturity is the ability of the group to confront one another directly (rather than talking about one another outside the group or avoiding discussion altogether). Cooperation replaces conflict in a mature group. Differences are still there, but the group handles them by adapting and problem solving. Disagreements are verbalized and dealt with openly. Group members provide constructive feedback for one another; and feedback is heard and used to change behavior. An overprotective or overcontrolling group leader can influence whether a group is able to fully mature or not.

Effective leaders act very much like group members and effective group members act like group leaders in this phase. Contributions are evaluated on merit, not on the prestige of the contributor. From this perspective, group leaders do not solve problems in the working phase, but see that problems get solved (Gordon, 1977, p. 43).

The focus in the *termination phase* is on evaluating and summarizing the group experience. Feelings of sadness, satisfaction, frustration or anger, guilt, and rejection or denial of feeling may occur. The longer the group has been together, the more intense and extended will be the termination phase. In any one session, groups may show behavior characteristic of all three phases. For example, the group may show some anxiety upon reconvening after a break of a week or more, until they reorient themselves to one another. A relatively mature group will then move into shared leadership. At the end of each session, especially productive ones, group members may show termination behaviors indicating sadness or reticence to end the group, or satisfaction with their work.

The leader elicits group members' summary and evaluative comments at the end of each session and at the end of the group. Some comments that have been useful are: "This is our last meeting; let's evaluate our progress." "I'm feeling sad that this is our last meeting; what are your feelings?" "What do you think we've accomplished as a group (today)?" "Let's evaluate our progress today."

This chapter will concentrate on group skills needed during the working phase of a group—the stage at which a group either will or will not achieve its purpose.

DECISION MAKING AND PROBLEM SOLVING

Usually decisions about group functioning are made by the group leader. Decisions about when, where, and how often the group will meet, how long meetings will last, and what the behavior limits will be are the responsibility of the designated nurse leader. The nurse who leads a group as a private practitioner must also decide on the fee-for-service. It is not usually feasible to open such decisions to group decision making, although the wise leader does allow group members to express their reactions to these decisions. Whichever decisions are nonnegotiable should be stated clearly by the leader.

Decision making by the group members occurs most frequently in task groups. Some decisions with which a task group might become involved include planning group activities; deciding whether to allow more—or less—time for a specific topic or problem to be discussed; deciding on the topic for the next week's discussion; and deciding how to handle group members who monopolize the conversation, pick on other group members, are silent, are new to the group, or are leaving the group.

Many groups will need to learn from the leader how to make effective group decisions by consensus. The first step in this process is for the leader to state the overall problem in clear and easily understandable terms. Next, the leader clarifies and elaborates on the various aspects of the problem. Next, group members are encouraged to develop alternate solutions to the problem and even seek out differences of opinion, since disagreement can assist the group to arrive at an effective decision when a wide range of information is presented. Throughout the decision-making process, the leader helps to keep the discussion relevant by making statements such as, "We're off the track now," or "Let's get back to suggesting solutions," or "We are discussing . . . now." Another step in effective decision making is to summarize the alternative solutions; this can be done verbally, or the suggested solutions can be written on a chalkboard or recorded by a group secretary or recorder. After summarizing the possible solutions, the group can test them out verbally and/or through action. As a decision emerges, the leader queries group members' commitment to it; for example, "It seems that the logical solution is. . . . What do each of you think of it?" The final step in the process is for the group to reach a consensus on the decision. Admittedly, arriving at decisions by this process is an ideal to be striven for; rarely will it be completely realized. However, one important result is that the group members are introduced to the process and the skills used to make effective decisions by consensus.

Sometimes groups become bogged down when attempting to solve a problem or make a decision. Koberg and Bagnall (1972) have provided *guidelines for problem solving, creativity, and goal attainment*. Methods discussed include: brainstorming, manipulative verbs, synectics, tell me stranger, games to develop belief in self, games to develop constructive discontent, games for developing wholeness, criticizing painlessly, and methods of acceptance.

Brainstorming

Gather together a group of 4 to 12 persons. Restrict the session to about 15 minutes and be sure everyone follows these rules: Defer judgment, ask everyone to suggest as many ideas as possible during the time alloted without criticizing anything presented. Avoid waiting for a new idea; as soon as one is presented, develop another one out of the last one given by changing it in some way. Avoid holding back; quantity is important. A follow-up session, using the same participants on the following day is a good way to pick up some afterthoughts.

Manipulative Verbs

This method uses a series of words to force the group to visualize the problem in unique ways. Some verbs used are: magnify, minify, rearrange, alter, adapt, modify, sub-stitute, reverse, combine, multiply, eliminate, invert, sepa-rate, transpose, unify, flatten, complement, bypass, stretch, repel, protect, integrate, and symbolize. For example, if the problem is "inadequate staffing," the group might discuss how to magnify the problem (so administration will notice it), rearrange (staff) by trying different staffing patterns, adapt (staff) by teaching floating staff sufficient skills to be of use on many units, and so forth.

Synectics

Synectics is the name given to a method of analysis, idea-tion, and implementation in which users find relation-ships between apparently different and irrelevant objects (Koberg & Bagnall, 1972). When using this method, the group follows three stages: in Stage 1, existing viewpoints are stated, the problem is analyzed, preconceptions are purged from the mind, and viewpoints are clarified. In Stage 2, direct analogy, personal analogy, and compressed conflict strategies are used to move away from the real problem and look at it from a new perspective.

In the *direct analogy strategy,* the group discusses how the subject is like other things. Questions such as, "How is the problem like an artichoke?" "How is the problem like flying on radar?" "What are the attributes or characteris-tics of this problem?" "What alternate characteristics could solve the problem?" For example, suppose a group is trying to improve the nursing care plan form currently in use. The group would first define the attributes of the current form: 10 pages, paper, typed, 8½″ × 11″. Alternate attributes might be fewer or more pages, erasable boards, computer-generated, 8½″ × 14″.

In the *personal analogy strategy,* group members role-play in various human, animal, vegetable, mineral, and abstract contexts. Each person imagines being transformed into some object, event, or abstraction. For example, becoming the client, the physician, intravenous tubing, restraints, siderails on a bed, a conference room, or a wheelchair. Becoming a linen room or linen in the room takes concentration, but it forces a different perspective on the problem.

In the *compressed conflict strategy* there is a search for problems within the problem; a problem is always made up of a number of little problems. Individuals often decide one of the particular subproblems is more important than any of the others; by identifying the other subproblems, a different perspective is gained. In Stage 3, new perspectives are brought back into relationship with the original problem and a new viewpoint and solution are designed. For more information on Gordon's Synectics, write: Synectics Education Systems, 121 Brattle Street, Cambridge, MA 02138.

Tell Me Stranger

It is always easier to see the solution to someone else's problem; solutions to our problems often escape us. To use this method, ask strangers or acquaintances how they would solve the problem. Avoid asking close friends and family members because they assume nearly the same personal feeling toward the problem. For example, if the group is composed of nurses, ask physicians, physical therapists, pharmacists, or lab technicians how they would solve the problem then bring their ideas back to the group for discussion.

Games to Develop Belief in Self

Sometimes a group gets bogged down because its members feel they are not making progress. Some games to develop belief in the group include (1) having the group write a column for the local paper describing how well the group solved some problem or worked together during one session, (2) having the group imagine it has won the prize for Most

Improved Group, and (3) having the group members compose letters to their families describing their thoughts and feelings about winning the Most Improved Group prize.

Games to Develop Constructive Discontent

Nurses often do not act because they fear "rocking the boat." The following strategies can be used to develop constructive discontent; the energy released can then be used to act: (1) Imagine your boss has accused you of participating in the overthrow of the hospital administration (an untrue accusation). She offers her regrets for having to fire you, pays you your salary, and immediately leaves on a 2-month vacation. What will you do? (2) Suppose your brain was transplanted into the body of your pet bird. You are the first and only bird who knows and knows she knows. What now?

Games for Developing Wholeness

Group members often feel cut off from their senses, and torn by various demands. Games for developing wholeness can produce a more integrated, whole approach to problem solving and decision making. Some suggestions are: (1) Blindfold the group and have each member identify three objects by touch, three objects by taste, and three objects by sound. (2) Have group members describe multisensory experiences such as walking on the beach, peeling and eating an apple, or taking a shower. (3) Have group members think of their left hand as their senses and their right hand as their knowledge; one hand feels and the other knows. Ask the group to write with each hand while concentrating on knowing and sensing. After several minutes, reverse, using the right hand to write and the left to know. (Lefthanders reverse the sequence.) Alternating back and forth will give practice in being manually whole.

Criticizing Painlessly

As group members make decisions and problem solve, they are likely to run into snags as they disagree with others' solutions. Have group members agree that whenever they are about to criticize one another's ideas they are to begin with two positive statements, state their criticism, add another positive statement, and finish with a ray of hope. For example, "You really have presented some good ideas. I like working with you. I wish we could stay on each other's beam. I notice you can adapt well when given directions. Maybe tomorrow we'll be able to stay on track together."

Methods of Acceptance

Accepting responsibility for a problem and a decision is sometimes hard to do. It took courage for the signers of the Declaration of Independence to sign their names to a document that changed their existing government. Group members can write their own Declaration of Independence by writing down why they believe that solving the problem is important. The declaration is written like a long motto. It can be xeroxed and presented to 10 interested persons.

Another method of enhancing acceptance is to imagine becoming the victim of all the worst things that could happen if the situation were not solved. Suppose the group wants to accept the problem of solving understaffing. Imagine that a plane crashes near the hospital and 500 accident victims are rushed to your hospital. Imagine that food suppliers go on strike and nursing is forced to bring in food and prepare it for residents. Have the group keep on this line of thinking until a very strong case for immediate action is built.

LEADERSHIP SKILLS

At one time, leadership was thought to be an attribute that, like charisma, was possessed naturally by certain special individuals. Now it seems more useful to think of group leadership in terms of a number of functions that need to be performed by some member in the group; the designated leader may, in fact, fulfill some, all, or none of these functions. From this viewpoint, the nurse can be seen as a group leader whenever fulfilling needed group functions. Thus, the nurse can be a group leader in a group for which the designated leader is a physician, a nursing supervisor, or some other authority figure.

Leadership functions are of two types: task functions and *maintenance functions.* Regardless of the type of group, both types of functions must be fulfilled in order for the group to work at its highest possible level of performance.

Task functions are directly related to the accomplishment of group goals; they include the following leader behaviors:

1. Getting the group going.
   (e.g., "Let's get started.")
2. Keeping the group moving toward its goal.
   (e.g., "Let's get on with our discussion of. . . .")
3. Clarifying unclear statements or behaviors.
   (e.g., "I'm not sure I understood your idea, could you tell us in another way?")
4. Suggesting ways to move toward the goal.
   (e.g., "We could spend a few minutes sorting this out before we move on to another topic.")
5. Pointing out movement toward or away from the goal.
   (e.g., "So far we've finished . . . but still need to tackle the problem of. . . .")
6. Restating more clearly what others have said.
   (e.g., "Let me summarize what I heard you saying. . . .")
7. Refocusing discussion on the task or on a small step toward the goal.
   (e.g., "First let's work on . . . , then . . . , the next step of. . . .")
8. Giving information.
   (e.g., "The group will meet from 8 to 9 p.m.")

Maintenance functions are directly related to improving interpersonal relationships within the group and may include the following leader behaviors:

1. Giving support to group members who are unsure or anxious.
   (e.g., "I guess you're upset about this, but give it a try.")
2. Relieving extreme tension levels.
   (e.g., "Let's role play this situation.")
3. Encouraging direct communication.
   (e.g., "Tell Mr. West what you were telling me, Mrs. Swanson.")
4. Voicing group feeling.
   (e.g., "I sense the group is worried about this.")
5. Agreeing or accepting.
   (e.g., "That's a good point.")
6. Helping the group to evaluate itself.
   (e.g., "Let's all tell what we've gotten from this group experience.")

In general, leadership skills are enhanced by using certain communication techniques. For example, *paraphrasing,* which involves restating what another person has said, gives the message "I care about what you said so I want to make sure I understand your idea." It is useful to preface one's remarks with a statement such as, "If I understood you, you said . . ." or "Did I read you right? Your idea is. . . ."

Behavior description involves stating only what was observed without commenting on the meaning or motive for the behavior. Behavior descriptions include statements such as, "Everyone talked today," "You interrupted Jane three times today," and "You already told us about your opinions today, John." Statements such as, "You must be angry," or "Why don't you listen to me?" or "You're just like my sister," are not behavioral descriptions, and they are likely to create discomfort and defensiveness in others.

Feeling description involves a direct statement of how one feels. One who uses this communication technique must feel safe and secure in the group, since sharing feelings implies a risk. Direct expressions of feeling include such comments as, "I'm nervous," "I'm angry," "I feel happy," and "I like you." Indirect expression of feelings is open to misinterpretation by others and should be avoided by group leaders. Some indirect feeling expressions are blushing when embarrassed, saying nothing or attacking a group member when angry or anxious, and changing the subject or the rules when irritated.

Validating is a technique that includes checking with others in a tentative way to see whether one's perceptions are correct. Paraphrasing has to do with verbal statements, while validating has more to do with hunches, feelings, and nonverbal processes. When attempting to validate, the leader avoids showing approval or disapproval of behavior and merely checks out perceptions. Validating statements include such comments as, "You seem nervous; are you?" and "I sense you're angry with me; am I right?" Effective leaders never assume that their perceptions are correct without checking them out; statements such as, "Why are you angry?" and "Why didn't you . . .?" should not be used before validating that the person is angry or did not follow through.

Feedback refers to letting group members know how they affect each other. Feedback is most helpful when it is specific, concrete, and based on empathy rather than on the leader's need to appear in charge. Examples of this technique are, "You've talked a lot today; let someone else talk," and "You've asked that question four times; what's that all about?"

TEAM BUILDING

Effective teams are the result of specific skill, knowledge, and hard work. Although it is not always possible to choose the people on a team, there is often an opportunity to influence the selection. Nurse leaders who want effective teams become part of the hiring and personnel selection process. Using a method for identifying individual differences and skills among team members is important. One system, the *SELF Profile* helps identify how team members learn, add to team functioning, and are motivated to work with the team (Jacobsen-Webb, 1985).

The SELF system identifies four behavioral types: (1) *Self-reliant* (this type may appear cool and distant, is precise about time use, willing to take interpersonal risks, prefers telling others what to do, is task-oriented, and uses few voice changes or gestures); (2) *Enthusiast* (this type is verbal, quick-acting, shows feelings and concerns easily, loses interest quickly, prefers to tell others what they *feel,* and is people-oriented); (3) *Loyal* (this type is more concerned about feelings than facts, is flexible about time use, is people-oriented, prefers to ask others what they are feeling, is cooperative, and appears warm and close in interpersonal relationships); (4) *Factual* (this type is cooperative, nonverbal, and low risk-taking; he or she may seem cool and distant when trying to remain precise about the use of time; prefers to work with facts and figures rather than feelings and intuition; needs time to study facts and make a decision; and tends to ask others what they are doing).

When building a team, it is helpful to have at least one of each type on the team. The self-reliant person can help conclude discussion, set the timetable, and push for decisions; the enthusiast will bring creativity to the group's work; the loyal person will make the work pleasant; and the factual person will supply the data and facts for decisions. Note that the same person may play different roles in different group situations. The categories are meant to be used to show which one usually dominates when in a nonthreatening situation. (Jacobsen-Webb, 1985)

Cohesiveness in a team is developed by increasing the quantity of connections among team members. Holding regular team meetings increases cohesiveness because interacting with each other as members of the same team strengthens the sense of being a part of that team. Nurse leaders can increase the sense of "team" by: pointing out how cooperation between team members contributed to its success, asking team members to help each other out, helping team members solve problems by using team time and energy, and asking team members to share their experiences with one another. A feeling of enthusiasm for the team can be enhanced by setting some worthwhile but attainable goals with the team; success in meeting the goals will increase team spirit. Even failure in attaining goals can be used to demonstrate the need to work together to overcome failure. Although useful in some situations, negative approaches such as identifying a common enemy and competing against other teams should be used sparingly because they set up win–lose situations.

An example of how employee competition at the worksite among teams can produce positive results was reported by Klesges, Basey, and Glasgow (1986). Four worksites were used; all were financial institutions. The bank presidents challenged each other at a press conference to see which institution could produce the greatest reductions in smoking among employees. The bank with the highest participation rate received a $100 prize; the bank with the greatest carbon monoxide reductions (assessed by breath samples) received a $150 prize. The bank with the greatest carbon monoxide reductions at 6-month follow-up received a $250 prize. The "grand prize" was awarded to the bank with the highest cessation rate at follow-up. A catered meal was served to the employees of the winning bank by the executives of the losing banks. To keep the competition going, employees wore buttons stating, "I'm in the Healthy Competition." A higher percentage of employees quit smoking in the competition condition (16%) compared with the noncompetition group (7%). There were no differences between the two groups in terms of age, sex, socioeconomic status, or percentage of employees who smoked.

As with other groups, team leaders must clearly define and negotiate their purposes, objectives, and member roles. Team leaders must also consider *delegation of responsibility* and criteria for assignment making. The two most important criteria are the ability of the team member to carry out the task and the fairness of the assignment. Nurse leaders may have difficulty in delegating responsibility; signs of this include: always being very busy, needing to be in three places at once, rushing from crisis to crisis, difficulty making and scheduling appointments with team members, team breakdown (i.e., the team falls apart when the leader is not there because team members have not been taught how to handle the team's regular functions), and verbal statements from the leader such as, "I'm so busy, I don't have time to do what I need to do."

Team leaders must ask themselves: "Do I have difficulty delegating responsibility?" "Do I really trust others to do the job right?" "Do I have a need to retain control and dominate others that is keeping me from running an efficient, growth-enhancing team?" "Do I withhold information from team members as a way of maintaining control?" The following example demonstrates a team leader who had difficulty delegating responsibility.

The head nurse of unit A was frequently seen running around the unit. She cancelled appointments with her team and was always complaining about how much work she had to do; she frequently asked team members who were sitting at the desk, "Get busy, don't you have anything to do?"

When the head nurse called meetings, she told the team, "I'm interested in your ideas, please tell me what you think." At first, team members volunteered their ideas; however, when they learned she never let them carry out their ideas, they became more silent in meetings, and stopped volunteering suggestions.

When a clinical specialist was assigned to the unit, she started to work with the team to teach them to share responsibility. A power struggle soon developed between the head nurse and the clinical specialist. When the two sat down to find out what had gone wrong, the head nurse realized she had been limiting the effectiveness of her team and increasing her stress level as well. They developed a plan to gradually let team members assume responsibilities for team functioning based on their abilities and performance in new roles. As team members were given more responsibility, they began to offer creative suggestions in team meetings and were able to grow and function at a higher level.

Inadequate staffing is a common and chronic problem in many health care institutions. Effective teams must confront this issue directly. Team leaders are responsible for pointing out to administration the inadequacy and the effects on care, reduced efficiency, poor public relations, failure to meet legal and accreditation standards, and inability to expand operations. If the administration does not respond, the team may go public and make appropriate regulatory agencies and the media aware of the problem.

To take such steps requires a team that will support one another and not back off from pressure. Team leaders ensure such support by using the team-building measures mentioned (Tappan, 1983, pp. 235–261).

PLANNED CHANGE

There are many models for planned change. Despite the model chosen, it is wise to remember that in a *systems framework,* change in one part of the system will affect the whole system. Thus, it is not always necessary to work directly with the target person in order to affect change. Nurse leaders who affect change will also be changed in the process.

It is common to hear nurses complain, "Nothing ever changes here. It was this way when I came and it will be this way when I leave." From a systems framework, change is inevitable; it may not be large-scale, sweeping change, but all open systems change. Change is repatterning of behavior. Some changes are barely perceptible, others are large-scale alterations in organization and patterning. All systems have the potential for change; it is this thought that nurse leaders must keep in the forefront of their minds when planning change.

Systems have a tendency to resist change and to maintain integrity and identity. Bureaucracies have built-in resistance to change; but even these systems change over time. Change is neither inherently good nor bad; some changes have positive effects on systems, others have negative effects. Resistance to change can often be a healthy response. The following example demonstrates how resistance can be healthy:

> University Hospital had developed plans for a new nuclear medicine laboratory. Nurses in the hospital picketed, protested, and wrote letters to the administrator describing the negative effects such a change might have on the health of clients and staff. They saw this change as a threat to their own and others' health and opposed it.

An *open system* responds to change according to the many factors influencing the system. Known positive effects of a proposed change is only one of the factors affecting acceptance of the change. This is why having only one change model at hand may result in refusal of individual or group systems to change. The following example illustrates how knowledge alone is often not sufficient to change behavior:

> Jerry, age 45, has emphysema due to heavy cigarette smoking. He recently had a lung removed. Despite the evidence to the contrary, Jerry insists he must continue to smoke because it is the only pleasure he has left. Attempts to convince Jerry of the dangers of smoking have resulted in resistance and lack of acceptance of smoking cessation.

Another factor affecting acceptance of change is the rate of change. Nurse leaders who expect their staff to incorporate a change rapidly given sufficient preparation are in for a rude awakening. Any change that occurs too rapidly is apt to elicit system resistance. Some of the factors that can affect system response to change include: the perceived importance of the change, the rate of change, the needs, values, and coping abilities of individuals involved in the change.

Often, including those involved in the change in the *early* planning stages prior to implementing the change will reduce resistance to change. Evaluating the system's probable response to change and choosing a model that will be most apt to influence positive change are two skills nurse leaders must have in their repertoires.

There are many models for planned change. Four that will be discussed are the: rational model, normative model, power-coercive model, and paradoxical model. It behooves nurse leaders to be familiar with all four models. The model chosen will depend on the circumstances and system involved. It is helpful to have more than one model to use in the event the first choice is not successful.

Rational Model for Planned Change

Nurses are probably most familiar with the rational model for change. Assumptions underlying this model are: people are logical and behave rationally; ignorance and superstition are the main blocks to change; once people become informed, they will adopt the change willingly.

One of the best known examples of this model is Rogers' "diffusion of innovation " (1971). This model is frequently used in health education. Rogers' model has three steps: invention of the change, diffusion or communication of information about the change, and adoption or rejection of the change.

The rational model is the method of choice when there is almost universal readiness for the change within the system. The following example illustrates a system ready for change for which the rational model is a good choice:

> Sarah, a nurse practitioner in an HMO, has been asked by several of her clients for assistance with selecting foods that will lower their cholesterol. Sarah consulted references for the latest information on cholesterol and developed an outline and several handouts on

cholesterol (invention of change). Next, Sarah contacted all the clients who had asked for information, surveyed records for other possible candidates, and announced in the HMO's regular newsletter and on a spot radio announcement (use of mass media for diffusion) that there would be a workshop on the subject in 2 weeks. Sarah also hung a poster and distributed fliers to her clients in the clinic for the next 2 weeks. Sarah did a 1-month and 6-month follow-up on all workshop attendees to find out if they had made changes in their daily eating habits as a result of the workshop (adoption or rejection of the change).

Nurse leaders can encounter a great deal of resistance to change when they choose the rational model for use with a system that is not ready to change. Sarah found change occurred in the clients who asked for information and were motivated to change; workshop attendees who attended because a family member or boss asked them to showed little if any change on follow-up.

Normative Model for Planned Change

A more holistic approach to change is provided by the normative model. It recognizes and deals with the influence of needs, feelings, attitudes, and values on efforts to change. Assumptions underlying this model are: all members of the system are active participants in the change process; rationality is only one of the many factors influencing change; the system can resist or modify change; education alone is not enough to implement change.

Two types of normative models are of particular interest to nurse leaders: the *Change Process Model* and the *Change Agent Model*.

Change Process Model

The Change Process Model was developed by Lewin (1951) and further developed by Schein and Bennis (1975). The Change Process Model is divided into three phases: freezing, changing, and refreezing. Lewin (1951) recommends an analysis of the system be made to identify forces for and against change prior to implementing the change process. For example, in attempting to assist group members to reduce stress, the nurse leader identified the following forces for change: participation in learning about stress management procedures, lip service to the importance of role modeling, and group members' ability to learn stress management procedures. An identification of forces against change included: potential threat to group members when giving up their old methods of dealing with stress, little or no previous knowledge of stress management methods, refusal of participants to complete between-class stress management tasks due to "lack of time," and lack of group participation in selection of class materials or topics covered.

Groups often need a push to begin the change process. There are specific procedures used to *unfreeze* the system so it will be ready to change; these include creating disconfirmation, inducing guilt and anxiety, and providing psychological safety. In the example above, the group had already come together as a group of teachers who planned to teach their students stress management methods; the nurse leader had yet to convince them to become appropriate role models in stress reduction methods, although they gave lip service to the idea.

The group leader brought research findings to the group detailing how role modeling was a powerful teaching tool (disconfirmation), indicated group members may not be doing the best job possible if they did not role model stress management (induce guilt and anxiety), and assured group members they would have ample time and opportunity to learn how to use the procedures in their own lives prior to teaching them to their students (provide psychological safety).

During the *change phase* of the process, the group leader encouraged group members to practice and experiment with stress management procedures (so it would become part of the system's regular patterns); provided a supportive climate (to reduce resistance to change); provided opportunities to ventilate guilt, anxiety, and/or anger aroused by the change process (reduce resistance to change); provided feedback on progress and clarified goals (reinforce change and keep the group on its task); preserved confidentiality (reduce resistance to change); acted as an energizer; and returned to unfreezing tactics when resistance arose.

The purpose of the *refreezing phase* is to make sure the change becomes part of the everyday functioning of the system. Nurse leaders who provide continuing education experiences for groups of nurses must pay particular attention to this phase to ensure participants do not return to their work settings and return to previous patterns of behavior. Providing follow-up workshops, interviews, letters, phone discussions, or peer partners with specific reinforcement skills will assist with refreezing in these instances.

When working with ongoing groups, the nurse leader completes the following functions during the refreezing phase: providing continued interest and support in moving toward integrating the behavior; delegating responsibility to group members; keeping the change visible by stating observed change, providing charts, letters, memos, newsletter items, and other concrete measures of change; intervening when problems in implementation of new behavior occurs; designating specific group members as peer helpers whom other group members can use as resources when the group is not in session.

Change Agent Model

Havelock (1973) and Lippitt (1973) developed a model with specific steps focused on communication skills and a good working relationship with the leader; steps in the Change Agent Model include: building a relationship of trust, diagnosing the problem through a consensus of opinion, assessing resources for change, setting goals, selecting strategies, and reinforcing change.

Normative models work best where there is little resistance to change and participants are open to being persuaded and can problem solve. Often, bosses or others may not be open to persuasion; at other times, normative models will not work well because there are conflicting values that preclude consensus, or when those in power resist sharing it with others.

The example that follows shows how one nurse leader used the Change Agent Model to implement planned change:

Tom, a nurse who worked with groups of high school students to prevent drug abuse, spent time meeting with interested students (build a relationship). He listened as they told him about drug use on campus. All agreed that something had to be done to prevent junior high students from beginning to take drugs (diagnose the problem). The group discussed the need for specific times to meet with the junior high students to discuss the problem, provide handouts needed about drug use, and disseminate knowledge on how to prevent drug use (assess resources). Tom shared the peer support model he had used successfully when teaching nursing students to support one another in implementing a fitness goal. He said he would be happy to teach the senior high students the peer support process. Tom suggested they look for a *leverage point*—a point where it is most easy to get movement toward change. The group decided to hold a Saturday workshop the first week of school to offer junior high students help with resisting drugs (set goals and select strategies). One hundred junior high students attended the Saturday workshop; most were eager to speak and ask questions about how the senior high students could help. Prior to the workshop Tom had met with the senior high "peer" group and helped them learn the peer support process; although he attended the workshop, the senior high students were in charge. By the end of the workshop, 50 student-peer pairs had been formed and goals for each pair had been established. Some students worked on learning assertiveness responses to being offered drugs, others wanted to obtain more information about types of drugs and their effects. Each pair had established a weekly meeting date and place (stabilize, consolidate, and reinforce the change). Tom also continued to meet weekly with the senior high peer support group to provide direction and support.

Power Coercive Model for Planned Change

The Power Coercive Model for change is focused on over-coming resistance to change. People's needs, feelings, attitudes, and values are recognized but not always respected. Assumptions underlying the model are: consensus cannot be reached through persuasive methods; when change is needed and the target system is resistant, power must be seized.

There are many different kinds of power that can be used including physical force, public embarrassment, loss of prestige or popularity (or threat of), money, nurse practice acts (legal power), public recognition and support, establishing oneself as an expert in the eyes of the public, using an idea or symbol that has meaning (i.e., Ghandi used the power of passive resistance effectively), strength in numbers (if all nurses united in one hospital, the strength of their power would be felt), control of access to resources (if a group of nurses seized access to money, communications, or information in a health care agency, they would have a great deal of power).

The basic steps in the Power Coercive Model are: define the issue and identify the opponent, organize a following, build a power base, begin an action phase, keep the pressure on, and force a decision through struggle. These steps are derived from Haley's (1969) and Alinsky's (1972) work. Both concentrate on the use of power by the "have nots" who do not have the advantage of holding high positions, great wealth, or other vast resources. The Power Coercive Model uses the sources of power most available to the have nots.

The example that follows illustrates use of the Power Coercive Model (Tappan, 1983, pp. 311–317):

The chief of the medical staff was being pressured by two traditional obstetricians and an oncologist not to allow nurses to teach their clients postpartum exercises or to talk with them about impending death—one client had been found weeping after a talk with a nurse.

The Chief of Medicine took his complaints to the hospital administrator who asked the Director of Nursing to ask all nurses to cease client teaching and counseling; the Director of Nursing refused and showed him a copy of the Nurse Practice Act. The administrator sent out his own memo ordering the nurses to cease teaching and practicing. The head nurse on one unit was infuriated and decided the issue was nurses' rights and the opponent was the administrator (define the issue and the opponent). The head nurse met with two of her nurse friends; they decided to collect signatures and send a reasonable letter stating their position to the administrator (organize a following). Signatures were collected and key people who signed met with the head nurse to plan their next move. They identified their power by the many nurses who had signed the letter (strength in numbers); the Nurse Practice Act (legal power); support of clients, most physicians, and staff for client teaching (public support); the fact that nurses were good at their work (expert power); and the potential to refuse to work and paralyze the hospital (threat of harm). Four nurses launched a campaign to publicize their fight and build support; buttons were distributed to nurses that said, "Nurses' Rights" (begin action phase). The nurses asked clients, physicians, and other nurses to call or stop by the administrator's office to tell him they thought he was susceptible to physician influence (keeping the pressure on), and to refer to the administrator as "Chicken Chuck." By using ridicule, the nurses hoped to keep the pressure on. The four nurses met with the Director of Nursing and asked for more direct support from her. Their next attack focused on making the administrator look foolish by obeying his rules and bringing pressure from outside the hospital. They stopped talking to clients. The Director of Nursing cancelled all prenatal classes and asked the local newspaper and radio stations to announce the cancellations. The president of the board called the administrator demanding to know why they were going to be the only hospital in the city without "those popular prenatal classes" and ordered the administrator to stop the public announcements. The chief of staff told the administrator to let the nurses get on with their work and stop being ridiculous so physicians could get on with theirs.

The nurses celebrated their victory with their following. They were asked to serve on a Nursing Advisory Committee to make recommendations about any policies affecting nursing. The Director of Nursing strengthened her position in relation to the administrator so that future policies affecting nursing came only from her office.

Paradoxical Model of Planned Change

The Paradoxical Model is based on the Brief Therapy techniques of Frankl (1967), Haley and Erickson (1973), and Watzlawick, Weakland and Fisch (1974). Some assumptions underlying the model are:

1. There are two kinds of change. *First order change* is one that occurs within a given system. The individual exhibiting the behavior may change, or a variation of the behavior may change, but the system remains the same. For example, a disturbed family may exhibit disturbance through a child getting low grades in school and high absenteeism. When the child is given individual therapy, he or she may stop the behavior, but the mother may then start drinking heavily. Both these behaviors are symptoms of an underlying problem in the family system. Only the disturbance has moved from one family member to another one.

2. First order change does not alter behavior patterns, but may reinforce them.

3. *Second order change* is change of change. The system changes due to taking on a new perspective on the problem or situation. *Reframing* is used to see the problem from a different angle and approach it from a new perspective. By using the client's language and perceptual system, the problem and solution are reframed or restated so the client can change.

4. System change is produced by dealing with the effects and not the causes of the problem.

5. Insight is not necessary to effect change.

Steps in the Paradoxical Model for change are:

1. Forget trying to understand the cause of the problem.
2. Determine the symptom–solution cycle.
3. Encourage resistance.

4. Define goal behavior.
5. Secure a commitment to change.
6. Set a time limit.
7. Prescribe the symptom.
8. Include a variation.
9. Reframe in the client's language.
10. Secure agreement to follow instructions.
11. Predict a relapse.
12. Demystify or disengage.

The example that follows illustrates one use of the Paradoxical Model in a group setting:

A group of nursing students had decided to discuss their fears of speaking up in interdisciplinary conferences. The group leader omitted exploring the past history of their speaking up and did not try to help the students understand the underlying causes of their nervousness in groups (forget understanding).

The group leader spent 15 minutes helping group members describe exactly what happened before they attempted speaking up in a group or in an interdisciplinary group. They described feeling a rush of anxiety, tightness in their stomachs, dry throats, pounding hearts, and cracking voices, culminating in remaining silent (determine the symptom–solution cycle).

One student said she would rather not talk about the problem and asked if she could just listen. The group leader told the student, "Sure, hold back until it seems all right for you to speak. Don't reveal anything until you're ready." (Encourage resistance. This gives group members two messages: It is alright to withhold, and that a time will come when they will feel alright to tell more.) The group leader then helped the group members define a behavioral goal of, "Being able to speak up in an interdisciplinary meeting." (Define goal behavior.)

The group leader asked the group to think for a while about their willingness to try a new solution to the problem, and said, "I have a solution in mind, but I will only tell you if you promise to carry out the instructions to the letter." (Secure a commitment to change.) The group agreed unanimously. Next, the group leader said, "Do you want the slow or fast method?" The group replied in unison, "Fast!" (Set a time limit. By setting up an either/or question about time, the group leader secures group agreement that change will take place— their only choice is whether it will occur sooner or later.)

The group leader continued, "First of all, I want you to go ahead and be nervous when you walk into the next interdisciplinary meeting. As you walk in, notice how dry your throat is, how hard your heart is pounding, and how your voice is ready to crack." (Prescribe the symptom.) "Then, instead of the thing you plan to say, announce, 'I'm so nervous I'll probably blow this, but here goes.' Then you go into what you had planned to say." (Include a variation.) Next, the group leader said, "When you try to hide your nervousness from the group, you are lying to them. By telling them up front you are nervous, you will be able to continue because your anxiety will decrease." (Reframe in the client's language.) Several group members had indicated the importance of honesty in dealing with others so the group leader reframed the prescription stressing honesty and truthfulness. The group leader then reminded the group that they had agreed to try out the solution. (Secure agreement to follow instructions.) The next week, several group members reported speaking up in interdisciplinary meetings without difficulty. The group leader warned them that a relapse was possible, and not to worry if they were occasionally anxious in future meetings, and to stammer and squeak a bit in the next one to show they were nervous. "You don't want them to think your opening statement is a lie, so make a point of showing your nervousness just to keep in touch with the feeling," said the group leader. When the class ended, one of the group members was heard to say, "I guess my problem speaking in interdisciplinary meetings just cleared up by itself." The group leader then explained the process of Paradoxical Intention to the group. (Demystify and/or disengage.)

Use of the Paradoxical Model requires a group leader and group members who are highly motivated, willing to carry out or develop a seemingly absurd strategy, are creative, and who have a sense of humor. Since the model is so different from the usual way most nurses deal with situations, it may be the last to be tried, despite its usefulness.

Choosing An Appropriate Change Model

In addition to keying change models to knowledge, attitudes, beliefs, and values, Haffer (1986) suggests using an adaptation of Hersey and Blanchard's *situational leadership* styles to choose an appropriate change model. This model shows the relationship between the amount of support and direction the group leader provides and the degree of ability and willingness to change exhibited by group members. There are four group leader styles from which to choose: telling, selling, participating, and delegating.

Telling is for low ability and low willingness to change. Directions are spelled out clearly and direct supervision including what to do, when, and how is articulated. Power-coercive rational models work best in these cases.

Selling is for low to moderate willingness and ability to change, take responsibility, and/or problem solve. Group members are willing to change but do not know procedures for changing. They are searching for models and will often go along with a change if reasons for changing are spelled out and there is some direction given. Rational methods are more likely to succeed.

Participating is for moderate to high ability and willingness to change. Lack of confidence or motivation at this level may lead to unwillingness to change. The need for direction is low and collaboration is high. Normative and educative models are most appropriate. A supportive, participative, nondirective style is highly correlated with success.

Delegating is useful when there is high ability and willingness to change. Group members are capable of independent action. Consistency and internal motivation are characteristic of behaviors. Little direction or support is needed. Group members can determine direction, goals, and motivation. When group members operate at this level, telling or directing is apt to meet with resistance.

SIMULATED EXERCISES

Each of the two simulated exercises includes an experiential and a discussion section. The suggestions for the exercises in Chapter 2 should be followed here as well.

EXERCISE 1   Decision Making and Conflict

This exercise gives the learner opportunity to practice group decision making and to assess conflict within a group.

Objectives
1. To develop skill in group decision making.
2. To develop skill in assessing symptoms of conflict within a group.

Procedure

5–15 minutes

1. The group or the instructor appoints a leader.
2. The leader appoints a timekeeper, whose duty is to assure that the task is finished in 20 minutes.
3. The leader locates two group members who agree to be observers for this simulation and gives them an instruction sheet to follow. (See pp. 89–90.)

20–45 minutes

4. When the observers signal the leader that they are ready to begin, the leader reads the following task aloud:

    "We are to take 20 minutes to decide on five criteria for mercy killing. When the timekeeper calls time, our observers will report to us what they have observed." Let's try to use brainstorming, manipulative verbs, synectics, games, and methods of acceptance. (Refer to text for ideas.)

    Alternate procedure: The group chooses its own controversial topic.

5. The timekeeper calls time at the end of 20 minutes.
6. The leader asks the observers to report their observations.

15–45 minutes

7. The leader then asks the group to discuss the following points:
    a. What could the leader have done to reduce conflict?
    b. What techniques could the leader have used to assist the decision-making process?
    c. What was learned from this exercise that can be applied in other group situations?

Observer 1

Your function is to look for conflict in the group. Record verbatim examples of conflict as they occur, using the observation blank below. When you are sure that you understand the items listed on the observation blank, signal the group leader that you are ready to begin. When the group discussion is over, you will be asked to report your recorded observations to the entire group.

(continued)

EXERCISE 1 (*continued*)

Conflict Observation Blank

Symptoms	*Example*
members are impatient with each other	
ideas are attacked before being completely expressed	
members take sides and refuse to compromise	
members disagree subtly	
comments are made with strong feeling	
members attack each other personally	
members accuse others of not understanding	
members hear distorted parts of others' speeches	
members insist the group does not have the skill to solve the problem	
members feel the group is too large or too small to work effectively	

Conclusions: an impossible task; conflicting loyalties; status seeking; personal dislikes; appropriate involvement in working toward the goal

Observer 2

Your function is to look for decision making in the group. Record verbatim examples of decision making as they occur, using the observation blank below. When you are sure that you understand the items listed on the observation blank, signal the group leader that you are ready to begin. When the group discussion is over, you will be asked to report your recorded observations to the entire group.

Decision Making Observation Blank

Steps in Decision Making	*Example*
states the problem	
clarifies and elaborates	
develops alternative solutions	
keeps the discussion relevant	
tests commitment to the emerging decision	
summarizes	
agrees to the decision	
tests the consequences of solutions	

EXERCISE 2 Shared Leadership

This exercise gives team members practice in assessing and changing leadership patterns.

Objectives
1. To assess leadership functions.
2. To determine alternate ways of carrying out leadership functions.

Procedure
1. A copy of the Leadership Functions Checklist is circulated to group members, preferably a few days before the next team meeting.
2. Each group member, including the leader, completes the checklist prior to a group meeting. The group decides whether responses shall remain anonymous or whether group members sign their names.
3. The group leader or a designated group member tallies the responses for each checklist and reports the responses to the entire group at the beginning of the chosen meeting.
4. The group discusses each item, identifying areas where change is needed. Items suggested for change are reviewed by the group until a consensus is reached.
5. The group fills out the checklist in a week or two and repeats Steps 2–4. This procedure can be completed periodically until the group is satisfied with its ability to share leadership.

Leadership Functions Checklist

	No One	Designated Leader	Group Member (Name)
1. Who begins our meetings?			
2. Who makes sure objectives are set?			
3. Who supports group members during difficult situations?			
4. Who helps the team make decisions?			

(continued)

EXERCISE 2 (*continued*)

5. Who brings in data to help our work stay relevant?

6. Who helps the group break down the problem into workable small problems/issues?

7. Who helps group members speak clearly and clarifies unclear comments?

8. Who makes sure the group keeps on track?

9. Who summarizes what has been said?

10. Who points out our progress?

11. Who voices group feeling?

12. Who calls "process" so the group will examine what is happening?

13. Who helps the group relieve tension?

14. Who agrees, accepts, and provides reinforcement?

15. Who helps the group evaluate itself?

READINGS

Alinksy, S. (1972). *Rules for radicals: A practical primer for realistic radicals.* New York: Vintage Books.

Cartwright, D., & Zander, A. (1953). *Group dynamics.* Evanston, IL: Row, Petersen.

Dyer, W. (1976). Group Trainer. In *Impact strategies for interpersonal and organizational change.* Provo, UT: Brigham University Press.

Eklof, M. (1984). The termination phase in group therapy: Implications for geriatrics groups. *Small Group Behavior, 15*(4), 565–571.

Epstein, C. (1974). *Effective interaction in contemporary nursing.* Englewood Cliffs, NJ: Prentice-Hall.

Frankl, V. (1967). Psychotherapy and existentialism. *Selected Papers on Logotherapy.* New York: Simon and Schuster.

Glasser, P., Sarri, R., & Vintner, R. (Eds.) (1974). *Individual change through small groups.* New York: Macmillan.

Gordon, T. (1979). *Leader effectiveness training.* Wyden Books.

Haffer, A. (1986). Facilitating change: Choosing the appropriate strategy. *Journal of Nursing Administration, 16*(4), 18–22.

Haley, J. (1969). *The power tactics of Jesus Christ and other essays.* New York: Avon Books.

Haley, J. (1973). *Uncommon therapy: The psychiatric techniques of Milton H. Erickson.* New York: W. W. Norton.

Havelock, R. (1973). *The change agent's guide to innovation in education.* Englewood Cliffs, NJ: Educational Technology Publications.

Jacobsen-Webb, M. (1985). Team building: Key to executive success. *Journal of Nursing Administration, 15*(2), 16–19.

Johnson, D., & Johnson, F. (1975). *Joining together: Group theory and group skills.* Englewood Cliffs, NJ: Prentice-Hall.

Klesges, R. C., Basey, M. M., & Glasgow, R. E. (1986). Worksite smoking modification. Potential for public health impact. *American Journal of Public Health, 76*(2), 198–200.

Koberg, D., & Bagnall, J. (1972). *The universal traveler: A soft-systems guide to creativity, problem-solving and the process of reaching goals.* Los Altos, CA: William Kaufman.

Koerner, M. et al. (1985). Communicating in the OR: Confirmation, part 3. *Association of Operating Room Nurses, 42*(2), 244–245, 247, 250–251.

Lewin, K. (1951). *Field theory in social science: Selected theoretical papers.* New York: Harper and Row.

Lippitt, G. (1973). *Visualizing change: Model building and the change process.* La Jolla, CA: University Associates.

Rogers, E., & Shoemaker, F. (1971). *Communication of Innovations* (2nd ed.). New York: The Free Press.

Schein, E., & Bennis, W. *Personal and Organizational Change Through Group Methods*. New York: Wiley.

Schmuck, R., & Schmuck, P. (1971). *Group Processes in the Classroom*. Dubuque, IA: William C. Brown.

Sheridan, J., et al. (1984). Contextual model of leadership influence in hospital units. *Academy of Management Journal, 27*(1), 57–78.

Tappan, R. (1983). *Nursing leadership: Concepts and practice*. Philadelphia: Davis.

Watzlawick, P., Weakland, J., & Fisch, R. (1974). *Change: Principles of problem formation and problem resolution*. New York: Norton.

Whitaker, D., & Lieberman, M. (1964). *Psychotherapy through group process*. New York: Atherton.

4
Special Group Problems

Among the more common group problems that the nurse leader will have to deal with are monopolizing, scapegoating, silence, the new member, transference and countertransference, physical aggression, nonverbal groups or group members, absences, and manipulation.

MONOPOLIZING

Groups are likely to have one member who talks excessively. In certain situations it may be reasonable to expect one member to do most or at least a major part of the talking in a group session. For example, when a group member is presenting special information to the group, it would be expected that that person would speak more than the others. However, when the purpose of the group is to share ideas, to learn from one another, or to make group decisions, a member who fails to let others contribute can impede group movement. Novice group leaders tend to become irritated by the overtalkative member and often fail to consider that such behavior occurs because other group members allow it to occur. A systems framework helps the group leader to see how one group member's behavior affects group functioning and vice versa.

Monopolizing can serve as a protective device for the group. The more silent group members may be anxious or fearful, or they may lack trust, and it is somewhat comforting to them that someone else will take responsibility for what happens in the group. At the same time, others in the group may show signs of irritation with the overtalkative person but have mixed feelings about interrupting. Meanwhile, the monopolizer may also have mixed feelings about doing most of the talking. Overtalkativeness can be an effort to decrease anxiety, or an attempt to establish a special relationship with the leader. In time, the overtalkative person will no doubt feel even more uncomfortable and resentful for being the only one in the group who is talking. In fact, then, monopolizing is a group problem that arises when one group member agrees—on some level—with other group members to talk and thereby to protect them. Unfortunately, while monopolizing begins as a protective device for both the overtalkative member and the rest of the group, in the long run, resentment among the group members increases and group movement will decrease.

In such cases, the knowledgeable leader will intervene, using any of a number of interventions that have been found effective, so that group movement can occur. Which intervention the leader chooses will be based on an assessment of the reason for the talkative behavior and also on how effective a particular intervention might be. Not every intervention is effective in every group, and the leader may have to try several before one is found that works in a specific instance. Also, leader feelings about the intervention chosen must be considered. If the leader is not convinced that a technique can be helpful, it would be best not to use it; once negative leader expectations have been conveyed to the group, the intervention will be ineffective.

One source of monopolizing is the effort of one group member to convince others. Sometimes an overtalkative member may go on and on merely because the group does not provide feedback. In such a case, the leader might provide opportunity for feedback with a remark such as "What does the group think about what John has been saying?" This will often quiet the overtalkative person and stimulate other group members to speak.

Another source of overtalkativeness is the attempt of one member to interest the rest of the group in matters that are irrelevant to the purpose of the meeting. Here, the leader could intervene by polling for consensus about what the group considers relevant.

Yet another source is the attempt of one group member to meet a need for recognition. If the leader concludes that this might be the difficulty, it would be wise to assess the group atmosphere to see whether it is marked by threat and competition rather than by warmth and support; if so, several techniques are available to the leader for decreasing anxiety and tension. Also, the overtalkative member can be counseled between group sessions; individual recognition might provide sufficient support to allow relinquishment of verbal control of the group.

When the leader senses the support and potential strength of group members, their assistance in dealing with the problem can be elicited by saying, "I think we need to look at why one person has been given responsibility for what happens here." This may draw forth statements from the group, for example, "I don't know what to say, so I let Alice talk." The monopolizing person might also admit that silence is bothersome. If the group members are able to verbalize their feelings, the leader can then work with these with such responses as, "It's quite normal to feel at a loss for words when new to a group, but in time you'll feel more at ease here," or "Let's try to work out this problem of getting more people in the group to talk; what could we do to make the amount of talking more equal?"

Often groups are not cohesive or cooperative enough to respond effectively to this kind of intervention, otherwise monopolizing would not have developed in the first place. The leader may therefore have to intervene more directly by saying, "Stop talking, Fred; let's hear what Jim and Stacey have to say," or "Everyone in this group has a right to talk; does anyone else have a comment to make?" or "Let's move on to something else now."

If none of these tactics is effective, the leader might consider asking the overtalkative person to leave the group for five or ten minutes whenever monopolizing occurs. The "time out" technique must be used with caution, however, since it can be perceived as punishment. But it does place responsibility for talking with the remaining group members, and thus has potential for changing group interactions. Such a tactic is an example of behavior modification (see Chapter 6) and will probably work best when the leader is not overly irritated with and rewards the monopolizing person each time his overtalking decreases.

SCAPEGOATING

Scapegoating is a process in which one or two members of the group are singled out and agree, consciously or unconsciously, to be the targets for group hostility or advice. Many times the behavior of those scapegoated has become irritating; however, there are ways for the group to deal with such behavior without resorting to hostility.

The use of a scapegoat is a convenient way for the group to negate responsibility for what happens in the group. Simply by blaming someone else, the members of the group can decrease their own anxiety and ignore their responsibility. Frequently, the scapegoated member sets up situations that evoke the group's anger. Sometimes the group is really angry with the leader for not fulfilling their unrealistic expectations, but rather than displeasing the leader, members "take out" their anger on the scapegoat. They may also scapegoat one member because they themselves feel worthless or inept and can concretely focus on someone else's weaknesses as a way to feel better about themselves.

Since scapegoating hinders group movement, the leader needs to be alert to its development in a group. The following comments may reverse the process: "We seem to be blaming Louise for our failure to progress; what is happening here?" or "Mary, you always tell Jerry he is wrong, but is it possible you have some critical feelings toward me, too?"

To deal effectively with scapegoating, the leader must be willing to accept anger. The leader needs to be able to accept verbal anger, resentment, or disappointment without trying to change the subject, to comply with unrealistic group demands, or to retaliate in subtle ways. By accepting group anger appropriately, the leader can help the group to learn that authority figures are human and should not be expected to meet everyone's needs, but that this does not necessarily mean that they are punitive or nonaccepting of others' feelings.

SILENCE

The ability to use silence effectively is a learned skill. Some silences are useful to group movement, others are not. Silence can be a group or an individual phenomenon. In either case, silence can have a number of meanings. Individual silence may mean that the person is holding back information or self in order to punish the group or the leader, may fear displeasing others, is in agreement, or is trying to escape talking because he is anxious.

When silence pervades the group early, it is often used to conceal that group members are anxious and unsure of what to do. Those who are least comfortable with silence will usually speak first. Often those who break silences do so because they think they are responsible for keeping the group moving. *Sad silences* may follow discussion of separation, death, or ending of the group. *Angry silences* follow angry interchanges and may be clues to hidden hostility or resentment that can decrease group movement. *Thoughtful silences* can occur after an especially relevant interchange.

In many groups there is a tendency to assume that the leader should break silences, and this may be most comfortable for an inexperienced leader. In general, it is best for the leader not to break silences unless they appear to be building into a power struggle over who will speak first. In this case, the leader might comment, "What's all the silence about?" Thoughtful silences help group movement and should not be broken by the leader. Likewise, anxious silences should not be broken by the leader unless tension levels seem to be highly disturbing to group members. Sad silences allow the group to grieve, reminisce, or resolve feelings, and they are constructive to group movement.

In teaching or time-limited groups, the leader may have to decide whether it is more important to break the silence in order to convey information, or whether the group could profit from being silent. Whenever the leader does break a silence, it should not be done to introduce a new topic, but rather to focus the group's thinking on the meaning of the silence or what happened prior to it. A leader who breaks silences frequently needs to examine why this occurs. Helpful comments after a silence include: "Silence sometimes makes people uncomfortable; does anyone have any ideas why this is so?" or "What are you thinking?" or "We have a couple of people here who aren't talking. Does anyone have any thoughts about this?"

NEW MEMBERS

Highly cohesive groups will have a stronger reaction to a new group member than those that are less cohesive. Regardless of the level of cohesiveness, group members frequently have mixed feelings about the prospect of receiving a new member into the group; they may hope that the new person will contribute positively to group goals, but worry that they may upset old patterns of interaction or compete for power or leadership. The new member will also probably have mixed feelings about joining the group: fearing rejection and hoping for acceptance, and wondering whether this will be a satisfying or a threatening experience.

The leader can help by meeting new members individually before they attend the first session. This gives the group leader an opportunity to explain the group goal, to state any standing rules for group behavior, and to tell the person when and where the group will meet and for how long. The group leader encourages new members to ask questions and to share expectations concerning the group experience.

The group should also be prepared for the change in membership. The leader can ask the group for reactions to adding a new member. This tactic might reduce the potential for hostility or rejection of the new member. It would also be helpful to ask members to introduce themselves to the newcomer and to tell a little about who they are and what has transpired so far in the group.

Close observation of the group on the day the new member enters it can help the leader to determine whether intervention is necessary. If tension levels rise, the new member can be put at ease with a comment such as "You'll soon catch on to what happens." If the group is hostile or rejecting of the new member, the leader can say, "I guess the group is upset about having a new member. Let's take some time to talk about this." However, overdisclosure can occur when a new member is anxious and uses talk to decrease anxiety; the leader must guard against this. Such behavior can break group norms and frighten or increase tension levels in members who have been part of the group for a longer time. The new member might also react negatively after the session and even decide not to return. For these reasons, the leader will find it helpful to redirect group interaction by asking other members to express their thoughts or feelings.

TRANSFERENCE AND COUNTERTRANSFERENCE

Group members tend to project aspects of former relationships onto current figures in the group setting. This
transfer of feelings that were initially evoked by parents or
other significant people in a person's life is called *transference*. Transference occurs when a group member reacts
toward the leader as toward a parent, since both are identified as authority figures. If the person's parent was harsh
and unloving, the group leader will be expected to be the
same and behavior that is warm and loving will tend to be
discounted. Or the leader may remind a group member of a
close aunt; this member may be extremely friendly toward
the leader—far beyond what would be expected in a brief
relationship. When the leader of a group is quiet, those in
the group who have had the "silent treatment" from parents or significant others may react with transference of
their earlier feelings of resentment. Group members may
transfer onto others in the group their feelings of love, hate,
competition, or even guilt that they feel (or felt) toward
brothers, sisters, husbands, or other family members.

Group members frequently try to duplicate family relationships within the group. Such transference can be the
start of real friendship or of arguments; they need to be
considered as the distorted relationships that they are.
Leaders may feel a strong pull to act out the roles group
members try to cast them in; to do so would not be a
therapeutic way to relate to the persons involved.

Leaders who respond to group members because they
evoke reactions reminiscent of their own earlier relationships are engaging in *countertransference*. This occurs
when a group member reminds the leader of past experiences with significant people who had acted similarly and
were irritating, were menacing, showed the need to be
cared for, were of a different race or cultural group (and
were therefore not completely understood), or, on the other
hand, who had qualities that were attractive. Because of
these past experiences, the leader is likely to react with

anxiety or a sense of immediate recognition when meeting group members who have styles of relating that tap memories of these past relationships. In such cases, the leader is likely to be unreasonably irritated by, fearful or overprotective of, underreactive to, or attracted by one or more group members. The effect on the group is to provoke anxiety and disruption of communication.

The leader needs to be aware of any overreaction to group members; to neglect to do so is bound to lead to leader and group anxiety and will impede group movement. The novice leader might try to deny the existence of countertransference reactions even though they seem to be universal experiences. Rather than trying to hide the existence of such reactions, it would be useful for the leader to remember that countertransference is an expected reaction that frequently occurs when helping people are highly involved with patients or clients.

PHYSICAL AGGRESSION

The leader cannot allow any physically aggressive behavior among group members. This includes touching group members who do not wish to be touched, throwing restricted objects, and hitting or hurting oneself or others. Such behavior must be halted immediately, and firm limits must be set so that all group members will feel safe within the group setting. In many adult groups, the leader will decide before the first session that touching will not be allowed; this rule is often set so that people will be encouraged to express their feelings verbally rather than through potentially dangerous actions. Other leaders will wait until physically aggressive behavior occurs, and then set limits.

For adult groups, a number of interventions is available to the leader. At the first sign of difficulty she can say, "No touching in this group," or "Stop hitting me. I won't allow you to hurt me," or "No throwing; somebody could get hurt." The rationale behind this intervention is that the leader demonstrates respect for self and others by limiting physically destructive behavior. If this technique does not work, the leader can gently but firmly restrain the member. Or she may ask the member to leave the group and return when ready to express verbally what is felt. Another tactic is to ask the aggressive member to sit next to the leader; often people who are physically aggressive are frightened. But if the leader is very frightened, this intervention probably would not accomplish anything. Another way of intervening might be to say, "Tell us in words what you're feeling." The leader might also ask group members what they think and how they feel about their fellow member's behavior. This can evoke strong reactions as members recall past situations in which similar behavior occurred and can lead to fruitful discussions. When all else fails, and if the leader feels comfortable doing so, she can turn to the physically aggressive person and say, "I want to help you, but I can't do much about it when I'm frightened and can't use my energy trying to be helpful."

Leaders in a children's group can first acknowledge the child's feelings; "You're angry and you want to hit me?" Next, clearly state the limits of behavior: "No hitting allowed here." Other channels for releasing anger can be suggested: "Here, hit this pillow instead of me," or "Tell me in words what you are feeling." Finally, the child can be asked about being restricted: "What do you think about not being able to hit me?" For younger children, leaders may use nonverbal methods: hovering over the child in a calm, protective manner, or using their own arms or legs to restrain the child's arms or legs gently but firmly. When relaxed, the child may be able to cry (in relief) and/or talk about his feelings (Pothier, 1976).

NONVERBAL GROUPS OR GROUP MEMBERS

Children or elderly persons may be less able to express their thoughts and feelings verbally in groups than are people of other ages. This does not hold true for all groups, however, since adolescents and young adults or middle-aged persons may also have difficulty expressing themselves verbally. Whenever this is a factor in group conduct, the leader may need to develop techniques for stimulating group interaction. Planning and implementing a group activity such as cooking a meal or taking a trip to a favorite place is one way to get group members involved in different types of interaction with one another.

When unsure of nonverbal or silent members' reactions to a group session, the leader can learn about their thoughts, feelings, and perceptions by asking them to write on a card or piece of paper a summary of the main things that have occurred during the session, or to respond to an incomplete sentence. Some stems for nonverbal groups include:

Today, I feel ....

Having diabetes means...

Being in this place is...

I wish someone would ask me about ....

The worst (best) thing that happened to me since the last
    meeting was..

The thing I remember most about our last meeting
    was ....

I like (dislike) this group because.................................

Once the members have completed one of the above incomplete sentences, the leader might collect them, select one or more, and use the information as a focus for discussion. Merely reading them aloud may stimulate discussion. If no one responds verbally, hearing the ideas of others read aloud can be useful and may increase cohesiveness. Before reading anyone's comments aloud, however, it is best to check with the group to make sure that no one minds. Keep members' comments anonymous unless members volunteer that the remark is theirs.

To stimulate group discussion, the leader can ask group members to draw pictures of themselves or of their families, or bring a living or inanimate object to the group to serve as a focus for discussion and nonverbal interaction, such as a kitten, a loaf of freshly baked bread, a plant, some flowers, or a picture. Using a picture that contains one or more people, the leader can ask each group member to tell what the person in the picture is thinking, feeling, or doing; this may initiate discussions about attitudes, biases, and other barriers to working together or communicating with other people.

Movement and structured exercises will help to release tension, build group feeling, and teach control of impulses. One group member may be asked to start a movement, and the rest of the group is asked to imitate it. This process is repeated, until each group member has led and has followed the movements of the others.

Even though group members may be essentially non-verbal in their interactions, the leader can make many observations about the group when activity is their primary focus, including looking for smaller groupings within larger groupings (who plays with whom, who leads and who follows) and for changes in these patternings. Relationship to the leader is another area to be examined—which group members withdraw, battle, ask for help from the leader, challenge others, channel or divert the focus of activity, cry, or laugh. Group members who can express their feelings and thoughts readily will still communicate during activities as one member tries to get another to do what is wanted, makes suggestions, threatens others, or carries out the activity. The leader can also learn about the various group members by observing the atmosphere in the group. Is it busy, apathetic, noisy, scattered in activity, aggressive, peaceful? How do members react to support, approval, suggestion, and limit setting from others? What themes of play or work can be identified, and how do they compare with normal growth and development levels for that age group? Finally, what individual styles of relating to the materials or activity can be discerned, and how can these styles be best described—that is, are they scattered, un-related, concerned with being enclosed or shutting out others, experimental, creative, secretive, attacking, disorganized, stereotyped in thought or action?

ABSENCES

Absences from a scheduled group session may be due to real factors such as car failure or illness, but they can also be due to anxiety and fear about what is happening in the group. Absenteeism may also be related to group size; when many members are involved, subgroups and time limits can prohibit satisfying participation. It can also be a form of testing group limits. The absent member may be indirectly asking "Am I accepted or missed?" In other instances, absence occurs because the group takes low priority in the member's life.

When assessing the source of absenteeism, the leader may find there is a need to reduce anxiety. The group can be polled to ascertain goal relevance for the members, create a smaller group, evaluate leadership skills, and/or open up the problem of absenteeism for group discussion. In the latter case the leader may ask, "How do you think it affects the group when everyone's not here?" The leader should also try to contact absent members via phone or letter, not in order to make them feel guilty, but to convey concern. Members need to know that their presence is desired, that they have been missed, and that the leader is concerned about them. In highly cohesive groups, a group member may volunteer to contact an absent member.

MANIPULATION

Group members may try to manipulate other group members, including the leader, to meet their own special needs. One member may be especially charming and helpful to the leader in the hope of being recognized as a favored child with special privileges; the leader may fall prey to this kind of seduction and, by rewarding compliant behavior, hope to get the group moving. Another member may try to put someone else on the "hot seat." In both cases, the leader needs to guard against rewarding or punishing the member who attempts to manipulate the group and say, "I notice that some of the members seem to be taking advantage of others in the group; has anyone else noticed this?" No names need be called; rather, the topic is introduced to help the group to understand how the group can be manipulated for one member's benefit.

SIMULATED EXERCISES

The two simulated exercises that follow each include an experiential and a discussion section. If the group is large, it should be divided for the simulation into equal-sized groups of not more than 15 members. The entire group can reconvene for the discussion.

EXERCISE 1 Nonverbal Communication

This exercise is designed to give the nurse leader practical experience in observing and using nonverbal communication modes. Gestures, facial expression, eye contact, body movements, touch, physical distance and proximity, posture, clothes and their arrangement, sign language, silence, vocal and body sounds, and objects all can be used to convey an array of messages to others. Nonverbal communication can be as influential as verbal communication. When nonverbal communication contradicts verbal language, a mixed message results, which is confusing to the observer. For this reason, nurses who wish to be effective leaders need to be aware of their own body language as well as that of other group members. Because this exercise allows participants to focus on nonverbal messages only, it encourages a deeper understanding of an aspect of communication that is often not examined in real-life work, supportive, and teaching groups.

Objectives
1. To practice conveying common feelings without the use of words.
2. To receive feedback regarding nonverbal communication ability.
3. To learn to teach others to be more effective in expressing themselves nonverbally.

Procedure
1. The group or the instructor appoints a timekeeper, who is instructed to make sure that time limits for each section are observed. The timekeeper is directed to warn the group when ten minutes remain to complete the task.
2. A leader is chosen by the group or the instructor for each subgroup.

15–45 minutes

3. The leader asks each person in the group to portray the following feelings, using only nonverbal communication:
   a. tension
   b. anger
   c. love
   d. acceptance
   e. fear
4. The leader intervenes only when a group member is having difficulty expressing the feeling. In that case, the leader asks the group, "Give some feedback about showing the feeling more clearly." The leader coaches the group to help each one express nonverbal messages. The group can be told to draw from experiences in charades, drama, dance, or film. Feelings should be expressed one

(continued)

EXERCISE 1 (*continued*)

---

by one, with time for feedback from group members concerning what is effective and ineffective in the member's presentation of feeling.

15–30 minutes

5. The leader asks the entire group to discuss the following points:

a. What is difficult about using nonverbal communication exclusively?

b. Which nonverbal mode does each member feel most comfortable using, and why?

c. What ideas does the group have about the reason for some modes of communication being used more frequently than others? How could more modes be used by each person?

d. What was learned from this exercise that can be applied in other group situations?

EXERCISE 2 Stating the Purpose

This exercise gives participants skill in formulating, verbalizing, and assessing others' presentations of group purposes or goals. By formulating and actually putting into words the purpose of the group within which the nurse will be working, goal clarification can be increased, and hesitancy in presenting the group purpose to the real-life group can be decreased.

Objectives
1. To practice stating group purposes or goals to a group.
2. To assess strengths and weaknesses of group purpose presentations.
3. To list important points to be considered when stating a group purpose.

Procedure
1. The group or the instructor appoints a timekeeper, who makes sure that the time limits for each section are observed.
2. The group or the instructor appoints a leader for each subgroup.
3. The leader appoints a recorder to jot down important points to consider when stating a group purpose or goal.
4. The leader asks each member in turn to state the group purpose for the group each is to lead (or be a participant in), as if each was the actual group leader speaking to the group. If some or all participants do not know the purpose of the group or even the group to which they will belong, the following hypothetical groups can be assigned: a postoperative teaching group, the family of an individual who will return home after a long hospitalization, a supportive group for the severely burned, a consciousness-raising group for men, a supportive group for people with epilepsy, a teaching group for new parents, a nutrition group for prison inmates, a teaching group for individuals with congestive heart failure, an orientation group for new nursing staff members, a supportive group for families whose children are dying, a supportive group for people with quadriplegia, a play group for preschoolers, an activity group for senior citizens, a social group for nursing home residents, an exercise group for psychiatric clients.
5. When each group member has stated a purpose, each of the other group members points out at least one thing that was good about the way the person stated the purpose and one thing that could be improved; then that group member restates the purpose, using the group's suggestions for improvement.
6. The whole group convenes for 15 to 30 minutes to list important points to consider when stating a group purpose.

READINGS

Andrews, M., (1975). Poetry programs in mental hospitals. *Perspectives in Psychiatric Care 13*,17–18.

Auvil, C. et al. (1984). Therapist self-disclosure: When is it appropriate? *Perspectives in Psychiatric Care 22*, (4), 143–144.

Bell, R. (1970). Activity as a tool in group therapy. *Perspectives in Psychiatric Care 8*, 84–91.

Clark, C. (1977). Nonverbal communication. In *Nursing concepts and processes*. Albany, NY: Delmar.

Consultation to groups in conflict. (1975). *Journal of Psychiatric Nursing 13*, 11–15.

Crawford, J. et al. (1985). Group psychotherapy benefits in multiple sclerosis. *Archives of Physical Medicine and Rehabilitation 66*, (12), 810–813.

Crosson, C. (1976). Art therapy with geriatric patients: Problems of spontaneity. *American Journal of Art Therapy 15*, 51–56.

Dinkmeyer, D., & Muro, J. (1971). Special problems in groups. In *Group Counseling*. Itasca, IL: F. E. Peacock.

Eisenberg, J. & Abbott, R. (1968). The monopolizing patient in group therapy. *Perspectives in Psychiatric Care 6*, 92–93.

Evans, C. (1985). First aid for meetings. . . . Follow the four steps of the nursing process. *Nursing Success Today 2*, 20–23.

Fishel, A. et al. (1983). Assertiveness training for hospitalized, emotionally disturbed women. *Journal of Psychiosocial Mental Health Services 21*, 22–27.

Fox, M. (1971). Talking with patients who can't answer. *American Journal of Nursing 71*, 1146.

Gosciewski, W. (1975). Photo counseling. *Personnel and Guidance Journal 53*, 600–604.

Hall, E., (Ed.). (1973). *The Silent Language*. Garden City, NY: Doubleday.

Jupp, H. et al. (1984). Group cognitive anxiety management. *Journal of Advanced Nursing 9*, (6), 573–580.

Pothier, P. (Ed.). (1976). *Mental health counseling with children*. Boston: Little, Brown.

Reed, G. et al. (1985). Bulemia: A conceptual model for group treatment. *Journal Psychosocial Nursing, Mental Health Services 23*, (5), 16–22.

Rubin, J. (1975). Through art to affect: Blind children express their feelings, *New Outlook for the Blind 69*, 385–391.

Schwartz, L. & Schwartz, J. (1973). Transference: The hidden element in your relations with patients. *Nursing '73 3*, 37–41.

Vidoni, C. (1975) Development of intense countertransference feelings in the therapist toward a patient. *American Journal of Nursing 75*, 407–409.

Whitaker, D. (1975). Some conditions for effective work with groups. *British Journal of Social Work 5*, 423–439.

White, E. (1974). Group Psychotherapy. In M. Kalkman & A. Davis (Eds.). *New dimensions in mental health psychiatric nursing.* New York: McGraw-Hill.

Zieger, B. (1976). Life review in art therapy with the aged. *American Journal of Art Therapy 15*, 47–50.

5
Beginning, Guiding, and Terminating the Group

PREMEETING PREPARATION

Much of the preparation needed should be done by the nurse leader before the first group meeting. Three major preparatory tasks for the group leader are: handling administrative details and relationships, making structural decisions about the group, and interviewing or notifying prospective group members.

Administrative Issues

Novice group leaders may think that the client or work group will be the largest system with which they will need to be concerned. In reality, group members will be greatly influenced by other systems such as family, community agency, hospital, and other institutional systems. Therefore, the nurse leader who expects to provide a group experience for clients must consider how (and whether) these various systems interrelate. Highly organized bureaucratic institutions such as prisons, long-term hospitals, and even schools may present the greatest resistance to innovative suggestions by a nurse who suggests that she lead a group within their walls. The nurse's first task in such a setting may be simply to locate the appropriate administrator who can grant access to a group population. It is important to note that although highly organized institutions may present the most resistance to the nurse as group leader, smaller community agencies can also be resistant to change.

The nurse may have to educate administrators about how nurses can function as group leaders in task, supportive, and teaching groups. Since nurse-led groups are a relatively new development in some settings, considerable restatement and reinforcement may be needed regarding just how the nurse can function in this role. The nurse leader should expect to spend a great deal of time and effort working through system resistance prior to and while leading a group of patients or clients.

Resistance may be decreased if the leader can clearly spell out objectives for the group experience and potential group content during planning sessions. The clearer expectations and plans, the less likelihood there will be later that administrators may directly or indirectly undermine group movement. Group experiences should be presented as a joint venture, and it is especially important for the leader to help administrators to specify their expectations of how she will function. Points that need to be agreed upon include deciding on whether administrators will receive feedback about group functioning and exactly how this will be done; deciding who will be involved in the mechanics of setting the time, length, and place for group meetings; and deciding who will enlist, convene, and retrieve group members, and how this will be accomplished.

In summary, the leader who is about to start a new group needs to consider the following factors:

1. The larger systems within which the group population exists
2. The appropriate administrator or authority figure who can give permission for the group to begin
3. The administrator's knowledge regarding how a nurse functions as a group leader

4. An appropriate way to communicate the leader's expectations and plans for a group experience, including objectives or goals and a potential agenda or list of possible topics to be discussed
5. The administrator's expectations about the group experience
6. How to collaborate with the administrator in deciding how information will be shared once the group starts
7. Ways to agree on a method to ensure smooth handling of the mechanics of group operation

Decisions about the Group

The first decision to be made by the group leader is the makeup of the group to be led. In some cases this will be determined by the needs and availability of client or staff populations, or by the nurse's job description or assignment. In other situations, the leader may have developed an interest in a certain problem area and may wish to lead a group of other interested people. If, for example, the nurse is interested in emotional reactions to the physical illness process, she may decide to start a group for people—either clients or families of clients—who are involved with such illnesses. At some point, the leader will have to decide whether the group is to consist of people with acute or chronic illness or with only one certain illness, whether it should be limited to clients of a certain age, and whether to include family members or friends who might be involved in care. Yet another point for the leader to think about is the way potential group members may relate to each other. If the leader suspects that most of the candidates will be withdrawn and monosyllabic, it will be more difficult to stimulate group interaction; if members who are likely to be more verbal are added, there is a risk of having these members dominate the group.

One guideline for deciding on group membership is that close friends and relatives should probably not be included in the same group, since they may tend to reinforce old behavioral patterns. All members of children's groups should be of the same developmental level; when exercise or skill is the focus of the group, the children should be of approximately the same ability so as to eliminate feelings of failure or the scapegoating of less skilled members.

At times, the leader will have few options as to choice of members. Perhaps only six or eight people who meet the requirements of the group will be available. If the group is to be made up of nursing aides, membership will be predetermined by the number of available aides on the unit. An in-service educator who plans to lead an orientation group for nurses may find that the group membership will be determined largely by decisions made in the personnel and nursing offices.

Regardless of how group membership is determined, the leader needs to consider the aspect of group size. Groups of 4 to 12 members are the optimal size when frequent interaction and group cohesiveness are objectives. When the leader is inexperienced, or when children or highly verbal or active adults compose the group, it may be advisable to limit groups to four to five members. Groups of six or seven, or even more, can be formed when there is more than one group leader, when group members are primarily nonverbal, when the leader is more experienced, or when structured exercises or learning situations are used. The leader should remember that as groups become larger, the potential for cohesiveness decreases since there is less opportunity for members to interact with one another.

The leader also makes the important decision regarding how often the group should meet. Again, more frequent meetings are likely to lead to greater cohesiveness. In a busy hospital unit, however, meeting more than once a week or once every other week may become a problem in terms of scheduling.

The decision about the length of group meetings is dependent on several factors—the leader's time and energy level, the group's attention level, the purpose of the group, and the group's need for a warming-up period. Novice group leaders may feel quite drained physically after a 40-minute session because they are not yet skilled enough to cope with the highly complex and stimulating atmosphere of group interaction. For these leaders, it would seem wise to limit group sessions to 40 minutes until the leader has developed the skill and supervisory abilities needed to deal with longer sessions. Children's groups may also meet for less than an hour, depending on the members' attention span. Some groups seem to require a warming-up period of 10 to 15 minutes for chatting and socializing before work starts. This may be a useful device, and the leader may need to decide whether the meeting time should be expanded to 1½ hours so that more work toward the group goal could be accomplished.

Once a time limit is set, however, it should not be changed whimsically or without discussion of the pros and cons with both the supervisor and the group members. This is important for several reasons. First, by structuring the group and keeping the time and frequency of meetings the same, consistency is maintained: Over time, it can demonstrate to the group that the leader is trustworthy, responsible, and able to stick to limits. Second, short-term groups are likely to accomplish more if they know the time limits of their existence. Groups in which the prevailing philosophy is "This group will go on forever, so why rush into anything?" will accomplish little. The leader who runs a short-term group can encourage more efficient movement toward the group goal by stating at the beginning and end of each meeting, "We have x meetings left to accomplish the goal." Lastly, a consistent time structure is important if members tend to try to make it necessary for the group leader to extend a session by bringing up an important issue at the end of the time allotted; in these cases, it is better not to extend the session, because it teaches the group to work within limits without waiting until the last moment to bring up important matters. To assist in this teaching effort, the leader can remind the group at intervals, "We have 30 minutes left today" or "We have 10 minutes left for talking today."

The total number of group sessions may be predetermined by the agency or the availability of group members. Groups that continually take on new members and lose old ones, such as orientation groups in professional agencies, or about-to-be-discharged client groups, may be ongoing. Planning or supportive groups, on the other hand, may be circumscribed and only exist until group goals can be attained.

Whether groups are ongoing or not, the leader must decide whether they will be open or closed. *Open groups* are those to which new members may be added. When the open group system is used, the leader needs to identify a population pool from which to draw additional group members. *Closed groups* are those that do not add new members, despite the fact that some may leave the group before it officially terminates. Neither is the better system, but deciding on this point is another matter for the leader to weigh and evaluate. In doing this evaluation, the leader may consider whether the potential population is large enough to support an open group; how and when this potential population could be oriented about possible group membership; whether introducing new members would slow movement of the group toward its goal; and whether the group could exist and work with only two or three members.

Group sessions should always be held in the same place, if possible. The meeting room should be private, uncluttered, well ventilated, have comfortable seating arrangements (preferably circular to encourage interaction), and be readily accessible in terms of transportation. The leader will have to decide whether smoking will be permitted. When health concerns are being discussed, it is important to consider whether the leader's own smoking (and/or allowing others to smoke) provides a useful role model of healthful behavior. Likewise, furnishing high-calorie, low-nutrition foods such as cookies and ice cream to poorly nourished group members is a consideration to be balanced off against the reward factor of offering sweets as an inducement to participate. Such a trade-off may be more easily resolved if the leader decides to offer fruit juice and a nut-and-fruit bread or some other sweet but nutritive combination.

No group leader can force group members to attend the group meetings. (However, in some institutional settings, staff members often bring people to meetings in wheelchairs or make special privileges contingent upon group attendance.) Staff are usually expected to attend scheduled meetings, but client care may interfere. The most the leader can do is to stress the idea that a group experience has potential usefulness and that for the group to be of the most benefit to all the members, all sessions should be attended by the complete membership.

The goals or objectives that the leader formulates for the group experience depend on the type of group and its duration and the agency constraints. Some agencies become quite involved and influential in constructing group goals; others leave this task almost entirely up to the leader. For some groups, the leader's purpose may be to help clients to formulate their own goals. Group goals are best stated in behavioral terms using action verbs that connote observable behaviors. When goals are stated in this way, both leader and group members know when goals have been attained. Some group goals that have been stated in behavioral terms include:

To role play job interviews
To practice colostomy irrigation
To prepare an ethnic meal
To state four purposes of breast-feeding
To plan health care for residents on unit 6C
To practice three alternative ways to express anger
To demonstrate effective breathing techniques for each
    stage of labor

To share thoughts and feelings about having diabetes
To develop alternative ways to handle other people's reactions to disability
To prepare staff for primary care nursing

When choosing a probable group goal, the leader considers how to state the goal in clear terms, and specifies the tasks that must be performed to accomplish the goal and some interaction processes that probably will occur or be encouraged among group members. Most groups have a number of goals; some are short-term goals, others are medium- or long-term. The importance of specifying goals is that they guide group action and motivate members to work in a specific direction. Some variables that can affect whether groups meet their goals are: (a) the extent to which goals are defined in clear, observable behaviors, (b) whether members see the goals as meaningful, (c) a cooperative group atmosphere, (d) consistency between individual and group goals, (e) small risk of failure, (f) availability of resources to meet goals, and (g) the allowance of enough time and flexibility to modify and attain goals.

Preparing Prospective Group Members

When selecting participants for a group, it is best for the leader to speak with each potential member individually. This interview may be either brief or extensive, depending on the purpose of the group. The leader may conduct more extensive interviews when concerned about balancing the composition of the group, or if the group experience needs to be explained fully to the prospective member. For example, prospective members of a supportive group for those with cancer may need time to learn more about the proposed experience and to react to the idea of being in a discussion group with others who have the same condition.

A short lecture or summary of learning content can be

given to those being considered for a teaching group. Written or recorded materials can also be used to give potential group members a better idea of what to expect.

Factual information about how the group will operate is given to prospective members before the first meeting of the group. "Group contract" is the term used to refer to the basic operating agreement between leader and group members (see Table 5-1). This contract can be either written or verbal; either way, it is intended as a statement of group structure and expected group behavior. Statements in the contract cover such data as number of sessions; time and frequency of meetings; whether the group will accept new members if some leave; member and leader responsibilities for confidentiality; how recording equipment will be used by the leader; limits of behavior such as attendance and physical aggression; specific expectations about participation, goals, and (if applicable) fees. The contract can provide both structure and safety for group members. People frequently enter a group with many misconceptions about what will happen during the sessions. The more time the leader spends discussing the contract before the first meeting, the better the chances that a climate of collaboration will be created. The leader should avoid presenting too much information regarding the contract in a short period of time, because prospective members who are highly anxious may distort or selectively fail to hear specific aspects of what is being said. No matter how detailed or how general the group contract, it is wise to give members an opportunity to express their ideas and feelings about the items. While preparing group members, the leader also encourages everyone to state what they hope to learn from the group experience or how they will benefit from it.

The group contract may not necessarily be used for a working or task group. However, it is useful to invite reactions and, if possible, to orient prospective members to the group goals, frequency, and duration of meetings, and to

TABLE 5-1   Written Group Contract

I agree to attend ten sessions with a group of other new parents to learn parenting skills. I realize that the group will meet every Monday evening from 7 p.m. to 8 p.m. and that I will be expected to attend each meeting at the University Center. I know that anecdotes of individual parents are confidential, and not to be shared outside the group. I understand that a nursing student will record what is said in the group as part of a learning experience in group dynamics, but that the recordings will only be shared with her instructor for learning purposes.

....
Group member's signature and date

....
Leader's signature and date

---

limits and expectations for member behavior within the group.

EARLY GROUP MEETINGS

During the first meeting of a group, it often becomes apparent that individual members have some goals that are at cross-purposes to the group goals. These individual goals are referred to as *hidden agendas*. Leaders, too, may have hidden agendas. For example, the leader may say it is up to the group to decide what its goals are, while having already decided on the direction in which the group should go. Or the group goal may be to share thoughts and feelings about having cancer, but one of the individual members may hope for a cure. Hidden agendas in supportive or therapeutic groups often reflect the expectation that the leader will provide special safety, protection, advice, or knowledge. Whatever the items on the hidden agenda, they can be detrimental to effective group work, and the leader needs to act to decrease this potential. During the first meeting of the group, the agreed-upon goal should be stated and the group given a chance to discuss it thoroughly in order to clarify misunderstandings any of the members may have about how to reach the goal. Hidden agendas that are unrealistic and discordant with group goals need to be examined by the whole group. The leader may say, "I wonder if we've said everything about this goal? Perhaps we could go around the group so everyone can have a chance to react to it." Although it may seem that undue stress is being placed on this point, novice group leaders can often trace later group problems to insufficient clarification of the group goal.

Once the goal has been clarified, the leader might restate it for emphasis, for example, "This group is for kids with diabetes to share with one another experiences they have had with others who do not have diabetes." In addition, the leader might start the group off by having them tell, in turn, what it was like when they found out they had diabetes.

Especially in supportive groups, but also in task and teaching groups, the ambiguity of the situation often causes a certain amount of anxiety. Therefore, members will use their usual means of coping with anxiety. Some will attempt to seek structure and reassurance by demonstrating dependency on the leader or on other group members; to prompt the leader to care for them, they will ask many questions, seek advice, or behave ineptly. Others may pair off to provide mutual support. Still others may deal with their anxiety by acting as assistant leader or teacher.

The communication in early group sessions is often stereotyped, intellectual, and rational, following norms for usual social conversation. This early communication structure allows members to get to know one another slowly; too high (as well as too low) levels of self-disclosure inhibit early group movement. Some common themes in early group meetings are trust, safety, and dependency.

The group leader attempts to create a climate of acceptance and comfort, and stays away from the role of the all-knowing, all-giving parent or "expert." Group members will repeatedly try to cast the leader in that role. The leader needs to see this as a form of dependency. When the leader persistently refuses to be the "authority," group members will probably become angry. Some anger, directed at the leader, is an expected part of the group process and needs to occur in order to enable high-level cohesiveness and relatedness to emerge. If anger is not expressed directly ("You're the leader, do something!"), it will often emerge indirectly. ("The staff here is not doing their job," or "The staff mistreats us.") This particular form of attack often startles the novice leader, who may jump in defensively or try to be the ultimate authority. Neither of these responses is particularly helpful. Instead, leaders can use their reactions of frustration, anger, anxiety, or guilt to "hear" and understand what is going on in the group. In supportive groups, the leader may do more than just understand, and may comment, "I wonder if the group is irritated with me because I don't have all the answers?" By helping the group to understand and verbalize its concerns, the leader helps the group to move toward its goals.

The leader can perform three important functions during early group meetings:

1. Develop a sense of cohesion and connectedness in the group.
2. Provide sufficient structure for group interaction in order to keep anxiety at a tolerable level.
3. Identify the basic norms for group behavior.

It is to be expected that group members will talk to the group leader more often than they talk to one another. Very early in group sessions, the leader can begin to promote interaction and connectedness by assisting members to talk to one another by saying, "I don't know. Who in the group has a thought about that?" or "Ask Jimmy that one," or "Tell Mrs. Lane what you just told me." In teaching or activity groups, the leader can promote group interaction by saying, "Show Sarah how to draw up the medication, Andy," or "Toss the ball once to every member in the group; you start, Wayne," or "Perhaps Mr. Edwards can tell us how he handles that problem." By not providing all the answers or doing all the tasks, the leader gives the message that the members are capable of taking some responsibility for what happens in their group.

Another tactic the leader can use to increase group interaction is to reward participation through verbal and nonverbal communication. For example, the leader might say, "You seemed unsure about sharing with us, but you were able to do it!" or "Learning to breathe efficiently in preparation for labor is difficult, but you've made progress today." Nonverbal communications such as head nods and eye contact can be used to reward members when they speak or participate.

In the supportive group, the focus is on encouraging group members to share their thoughts, feelings, and reactions to crises, health conditions, or interpersonal relationships. A discussion or teaching group has a different kind of focus and structure. Since there must be a shared understanding of the language that is to be used, terms and concepts may need to be defined. The leader may ask members to draw up a list of words or concepts they do not fully understand. Part of the session can then be devoted to clarifying the meanings of the words and to checking to see that all members understand the terms.

As in other groups, the goals and objectives for teaching and discussion groups should be clearly stated. Since there may be new goals for each session, the leader should state the goal at the beginning of each meeting. Time should be set aside for discussion of each topic or agenda item. The leader may appoint a timekeeper to see that sufficient time is spent on each topic. The group is encouraged to help decide the priority of items to be discussed. The leader can help members to integrate new information by relating material to previous topics, by comparing and contrasting new and old information, and by summarizing and reviewing. Time needs to be allowed for application of new learnings or decisions. Depending on the type of group, members can be asked to identify the implications of the day's session for their lives, work, and/or their relationships with others. At the end of a session, group members can be asked to tell how or whether the session has been useful and to suggest topics for the next session.

Regardless of the stated purpose of the group, the leader tries to encourage members to share their common problems or interests. One of the major benefits of any group experience is learning that others are struggling with the same difficulties or decisions. The leader can point out common issues or problems and suggest that "these are important things for us to discuss at some point." In beginning groups, the members may not be ready to discuss the issues, but by merely indicating their importance, the leader opens the door for discussion at a later date.

GUIDING THE GROUP

As the group progresses, the leader continues to be a role model for clear, effective communication (see Chapter 2): being adept at revising goals as work progresses or as circumstances within the group change, teaching group members to share leadership. By summarizing what occurs in the group sessions, the leader teaches group members how to organize group experiences in a meaningful way; for example: "Today we've covered how to sterilize syringes," and "We're moving closer to a decision," and "I wonder if we haven't been talking about feeling angry because several members have left the group." As the group begins to take more responsibility, the leader can ask one member to summarize what happened in a particular session. The leader also teaches the group how to clarify thoughts and feelings; for example, "Tommy, you seem to be expressing anger; am I right?" or "I think you're both making the same point about disliking overtalkativeness."

The group can also be taught to solve problems, using clarification of the problem as the first step. "The problem seems to be that we need to decide on a topic of next week," or "Barry could use some help from the group in drawing up the medication." Once the problem has been clarified, the leader can ask the members to volunteer their ideas about how to solve the problem and then guide them in testing out or thinking through the possible results of each solution suggested.

A few noisy group members can prevent the group from reaching its goals. In a supportive group, the leader might ask the others to deal with the problem by saying, "Jack and Franny are forming their own group; what do you think is happening there?" In a teaching group, the leader might ask the noisy members to demonstrate a procedure or give their suggestions about the topic being discussed. In a group of elderly patients, the leader needs to assess whether the noisy pair is temporarily disoriented; if this is the case, the leader might ask them to try to listen to what is being said, or may provide them with written or verbal orientation to the focus of the group's interaction at that moment.

As the group begins to move into the working phase, members feel concern about their position in relation to the leader and other group members. Also, there is less need for control and social acceptability; this is evidenced by the use of slang, swearing, and informality; and the ability to deal with more complex issues. Depending on the type of group, the leader will observe other signs that the working phase has been entered. Often, members become more involved in sharing and intimacy issues; they seem to be testing out how much they want to reveal about themselves and how close they wish to be to others. Cohesiveness increases, along with a sense of respect and acceptance of self and others, and there is more sharing of personal data and reactions to others in the group. In testing to find the limits of interdependency, independent group members may en-

TABLE 5-2   Early and Later Group Behaviors

Orientation Phase	Working Phase
Dependency on the leader	Interdependency and shared leadership
Anger that the leader is not omniscient or omnipotent	Increased intimacy and sharing
Attempts to play assistant leader	Conflict between members and/or with the leader
Stereotyped, intellectual-rational, and socially acceptable conversation	Conversation on a deeper, less superficial level
Learning about others' similarities	Increased sense of respect and acceptance of other group members
Refining group goals	Collaborative effort in identifying and dealing with group issues

gage in conflict with one another or in direct or indirect war with the leader. It is important that the leader does not take sides or make judgments about who is right or who started an argument. Also, the leader must be vigilant about not giving in to the tendency to retaliate when group members challenge her authority. Although at this stage there appears to be a definite shift in behavior, some of the behaviors typical of the working phase may appear in early group meetings (see Table 5-2).

Table 5-3 shows leader behaviors that can be effective in moving the group from the orientation to the working phase.

TERMINATING THE GROUP

The process of terminating a group is both a group and an individual task. The entire group may disband, or several members may leave the group at one time. When termination is handled effectively, members can learn how to deal

TABLE 5-3 Some Effective Leader Behaviors

Techniques	Examples
Reflection	"You feel . . .?"
Deflection	"What do group members think about that?"
Clarification	"I wonder if you're asking the group for assistance, Mrs. Tanner?"
Asking for group reaction	"How do group members feel about not meeting last week?"
Increasing cohesiveness	"Many of you seem to be expressing an interest in changing the group goal."
Promoting interaction	"I don't know; ask Tom."
Exploring	"Tell us more about that."
Teaching decision making	"As I see it, the problem is to decide on an activity; let's pool our ideas. Who will start?"
Summarizing	"So far we've talked about sterilizing equipment, but not about drawing up medication."

with the separation from others that occurs in many life situations. The ability to say goodbye and move on to other relationships is a skill some people have never learned.

Early in group experiences it is not unusual for members to drop out, because they feel they do not fit in with the group, their expectations are not met, they have been scapegoated by others, they fear success or intimacy, or they have become part of a subgroup that decides to leave. Generally, the leader can make leaving most therapeutic by making goodbyes explicit; for example, by asking, "John is leaving the group; how do you feel about this?" When this is done, there is less chance for unfinished business concerning leave-taking and separation. Especially in supportive groups, it is important for the leader to help the leaving member and the group examine the meaning of separation.

Increased understanding can reduce the possibility that both those who leave and those who are left will feel they have failed or been rejected. Instead, the leaving of individual members can be explained as being due to unfitness, poor timing, external pressures, or unreadiness for a group experience. When group members leave a group because they have benefited from and grown through the experience, the termination is less abrupt and can be dealt with in several sessions of the group.

Even when handled well, termination can be anxiety-provoking when it evokes unresolved feelings about previous separations. Some people find it easier to leave the group; others are more comfortable when they are the ones being left. Hopefully, a group experience can help members to be comfortable both with leaving and with being left. Feelings that commonly occur in all types of groups when they end or when group members leave include sadness, anger, rejection, longing, relief, and accomplishment.

In some termination situations, members may attempt to continue the group experience by bringing up new problems or crises for discussion. However, setting new goals or starting new activities when termination is near is not a useful procedure. Rather, the leader can say something like, "This is our last session, and we can't begin to deal with such a complex problem now; we can make better use of our time by discussing our thoughts and feelings about the group experience we have shared." The leader may wish to continue the group; in that case, reluctance to separate should be examined outside the group, preferably with a supervisor or experienced peer.

Termination can be used by the group as a time for review, just as the end of each session can be thought of as a minitermination when thoughts, feelings, and accomplishments are summarized. Group members may also use these times to get in touch with unresolved feelings connected with past separations. They may find it difficult to share these feelings, but they should have an opportunity to do so. Leaders can take the initiative by sharing their own reflections on the ending or separation and by reviewing the group experience from her point of reference. This may give the group members encouragement to share their own reactions. Some group leaders ask for written evaluations or summaries from group members. Whatever method is used, it is the leader's responsibility to provide direction for the group about the way to end a group experience. It is also the leader's responsibility to explore his or her own reactions to the ending of a group or the leave-taking of group members; once these are identified, there is less likelihood of over- or underreactions to terminations.

SIMULATED EXERCISES

Each of the two simulated exercises that follow simulates one session of an actual group meeting. A list of questions to be discussed following completion of the exercises can be used to tie theory to practice. Group members may wish to record on tape either or both simulations and play back the recording to help them answer the discussion questions. If the exercises are completed without an instructor or supervisor present, a later discussion session should be held with a more experienced group leader present.

Each participant should have a copy of this book, if possible, or one or more books can be passed around to enable each person to read the designated material.

EXERCISE 1   A Simulated Supportive Group for Cancer Clients and Their Families

This intermediate- to advanced-skill exercise is designed to give the nurse a group experience that simulates some group processes that might occur during one supportive group session. In this simulation, group members role-play communication skills, leadership, anger, dependency, monopolizing, silence, new members, helplessness/hopelessness, and denial. The person who is the designated leader will have practice in leading this simulated group. The other participants will be able to assess how the designated leader led, how this may compare or contrast with their own group leader experiences, how it might feel to be in this type of supportive group, and what problems could be anticipated in a real-life supportive group.

Between nine and fourteen members can play in each simulated group. If more than fourteen people are available, divide learners into groups of between nine and fourteen and begin a new simulation.

Objectives
1. To provide skill practice as leader of a supportive group for one or more participants.
2. To assess communication skills, leadership, anger, dependency, monopolizing, silence, the entrance of a new member, helplessness/ hopelessness, and denial as they might occur in a real-life supportive group.
3. To examine alternative ways of dealing with typical group processes.

Procedure
    1. Seat the group members in a circle.
    2. The group appoints a timekeeper, who times the experiential supportive group to run for 20 minutes and the post-meeting discussion group to run for no more than two hours (the group should spend no more than 15 minutes on each discussion question). The timekeeper may also be assigned to run the tape recorder and/or take notes, depending on the group's decision.
    3. The group or instructor appoints a leader for each group of nine to fourteen members. The leader takes the leader role in the simulation (page 135), appoints or asks for volunteers to play the following roles, and assigns each to read her role description only on the indicated pages in this book:
        a. dependency role (1–2 players), page 135;
        b. monopolizing role (1 player), page 135;

(continued)

EXERCISE 1 (*continued*)

c. denial role (1–2 players), page 135;
d. silent role (1–2 players), page 135;
e. new member role (1 player), page 135;
f. anger role (1–2 players), page 136;
g. helplessness/hopelessness role (1–2 players) page 136.

20 minutes

4. When group members have read their role descriptions on the designated pages, the leader starts the group by saying, "Perhaps each person could tell why they joined this group. Who would like to begin?" The group simulation then continues for 20 minutes.

5. When the timekeeper calls time, the leader or a volunteer from the group leads a group discussion about each of the behaviors enacted, focusing it on the following points:

15 minutes maximum

a. How did the role leader deal with the person who played the denial role? Was it effective? How else could the leader have handled the situation?

15 minutes maximum

b. How did the role leader deal with the person who played the anger role? Was it effective? How else could the leader have handled the situation?

15 minutes maximum

c. How did the role leader deal with the person who played the helplessness/hopelessness role? Was it effective? How else could the leader have handled the situation?

15 minutes maximum

d. How did the role leader deal with the person who played the dependency role? Was it effective? How else could the leader have handled the situation?

15 minutes maximum

e. How did the role leader handle the overtalkative person? Was it effective? How else could the leader have handled the situation?

15 minutes maximum

f. How did the role leader deal with the silent person? Was it effective? How else could the leader have handled the situation?

15 minutes maximum

g. How did the role leader deal with the person who played the new member? Was it effective? How else could the leader have handled this situation?

15 minutes or more

h. How did the leader accomplish the four assigned tasks?

1. Starting the group: Think of three other ways that could have been used to start this group.

2. Keeping group members talking to one another: Describe comments a group leader might make to encourage interaction among group members.

3. Drawing similarities between group members: Make three statements designed to increase cohesiveness by pointing out group members' similarities in the simulation in which you have just participated.

4. Ending the group: State one or two other ways to end a group.

Variations: 1. Group members change roles and replay the simulation.

2. Add the roles of personal reactions and dependency, deleting other roles you have already mastered.

Role Descriptions

A SIMULATED SUPPORTIVE GROUP FOR CANCER CLIENTS AND THEIR FAMILIES

Group Leader Role

Your role has four parts: starting the group action, keeping the members talking to one another instead of you doing all the talking ("Tell the group that" or "Ask if someone else has an answer for that question"), summarizing what has been said ("Mr. S seems angry, while Mrs. T seems to feel hopeless"), drawing similarities ("Everyone seems to have strong feelings about this"), and terminating the group session. ("Our discussion time is up for tonight; see you Thursday night at seven.") Before you begin this simulation, decide whether the group will be composed of patients, families, or a combination of both.

Monopolizing Role

Your role is to continue talking whenever you can. Keep trying to convince the group that you know all about the cause and treatment of cancer.

Denial Role

Your role is to deny the fact that your spouse (or you) is dying of cancer. Whenever anyone in the group starts expressing anger or helplessness, make comments such as, "Don't get so upset," or "Things will get better," or "Cheer up; it's always darkest before the dawn."

Silent Role

Your role is to remain silent throughout this simulation. Observe how the others and especially the leader react to you.

New Member Role

Leave the group before the simulation begins. Come back and join the group in exactly ten minutes.

(continued)

EXERCISE 1 (*continued*)

Anger Role

Your role is to be angry because you (or a family member) are dying from cancer. Whenever you speak, make sure you express irritation. Make comments such as, "How can this happen to me?!" or "How can you sit there so calmly when people are dying?" or "God is punishing me," or "That's a stupid remark."

Helplessness/Hopelessness Role

Your role is to feel helpless and hopeless. Make comments such as, "It's no use; nothing can be done," or "This group can't help me," and "What's the use of talking anyway?"

Variations:

Personal Reactions Role

Imagine someone in your family is dying of cancer. Play the role you think you would play if this occurred.

Dependency Role

Your role is to seek direction from other members in the group, especially the leader. Look at the leader frequently, and make comments such as, "We don't know what this group is for," and "Tell us what to do," or "How can we cope with this problem; it's so overwhelming?"

EXERCISE 2   A Simulation of a Health Team Meeting

This exercise is designed to give the nurse a group experience that simulates some of the group processes that might occur during one task group session: apathy, conflict, decision making, and leadership. It gives the learner an opportunity to "get the feel" of how these group processes operate by examining and analyzing them in a relatively safe, standardized environment. At least 6 (and no more than 11) members act out this simulated exercise or those suggested as variations.

Objectives
1. To allow skill practice as leader of a task group.
2. To practice leadership skills, even though one is not the designated leader.
3. To assess the processes of apathy, conflict, decision making, and leadership as they might occur in an actual task group.
4. To examine alternative ways of dealing with the typical task group processes.

Procedure
1. Seat the group in a circular arrangement.
2. The group appoints a timekeeper, who times the experiential task group to run for 30 minutes and the postsimulation discussion to end after 20 minutes.
3. The group or instructor appoints a leader for each group of six to eleven members who use the simulation. The leader appoints members or asks for volunteers to play the following roles, assigns each to read the role description as presented in this book, and warns each not to read the others' role descriptions:
   a. apathy role (at least 2 players), page 139;
   b. conflict role (1–2 players), page 139;
   c. decision making role (1–2 players), page 139;
   d. leadership role (1 player; designated by group or leader), page 138.
4. When the group members have read their role descriptions, the leader says, "My role is team leader for this group. We are to plan health care for 50 clients and their families. Since we've not worked together before, we might start out by deciding how we will proceed to develop health care plans for these people. Who has some ideas about how to proceed?"
5. The simulation continues until the timekeeper calls time.

(*continued*)

EXERCISE 2 (*continued*)

6. After time has been called, the leader (or a volunteer from the group) leads the entire group in a discussion of each of the behaviors enacted, focusing on a discussion of each of the following points:

a. How did the leader deal with the apathetic role players? Was it effective? How else could the leader have handled the situation?

b. How did the team leader deal with the members who displayed conflict? Was it effective? How else could the leader have handled the situation?

c. How did the leader deal with group members who tried to assist with decision making? Was it effective? How else could the leader have enlisted their help?

d. How well did the leader lead? Did others in the group provide leadership functions? List five important leadership functions, and discuss whether they were adequately provided.

e. Have each participant tell what she learned from this exercise and how it can be applied in other task group situations.

Variations: 1. Group members change roles and replay the simulation.

2. Add the roles of pet project, do-gooder, and/or anticommittee, deleting other roles you have already mastered.

Role Descriptions

A SIMULATION OF A HEALTH TEAM MEETING

Leader Role

Try to fulfill both task and maintenance functions in the group. Try to keep the group moving toward its goal, clarify unclear statements, suggest ways of moving toward the goal, point out movement toward or away from the goal, summarize what others have said, give the group the information it needs to complete its task, and suggest small steps toward the task, such as writing down suggestions given today as a basis for the next meeting's agenda. In fulfilling your maintenance functions, give support to unsure group members, relieve tension, encourage direct communication, voice group feeling, accept group members' ideas, and help the group to evaluate its progress.

Apathy Role

When the simulation begins, yawn frequently, and pretend you are falling asleep. Squirm in your chair, and whisper to other group members. Make frequent suggestions to adjourn the meeting, and refuse to take any responsibility for decision making.

Conflict Role

Express impatience with others' comments. Make derogatory comments, such as "baloney" or "that's a crock!" Insist that the group does not know what it is doing or that the group needs an expert to help figure out this planning. Disagree with the team leader whenever you can. Accuse others of not understanding your point of view. Claim that only you know the best way to care for patients and that others are "very poor nurses" and "incompetent practitioners."

Decision Making Role

Try to restate the problem whenever you think others are off the track by saying, "Let's get back to our job," or "You're off the track." If you forget the group goal, ask the team leader to restate it. Clarify or elaborate others' comments with statements such as, "Are you saying that . . .?" and, "I'd like to add to your idea; what about. . . ." Summarize what has happened every five or ten minutes; for example, make statements such as "Gene has an idea he wants to push, but I'm not sure it's what the rest of us are getting at" or "So far we have decided (or have not decided) to do. . . ." Test to see others' commitment to emerging decisions by saying, "How many agree with the suggestion to. . . .?"

Variations

Pet Project Role

Imagine you have a pet project, such as consumer advocacy, clients' rights, or preventive health care. Use this team meeting to try to interest others in your pet project. Cite imaginary facts and fallacies related to your pet project. Be sure not to assist the group whose task is to plan health care for the assigned group of patients and families.

Do-Gooder Role

Imagine yourself as a do-gooder, novice nurse leader. Make grandiose plans for health care, without considering restrictions of time, money, or energy.

Anticommittee Role

Imagine you are someone who hates committee meetings and who has had negative experiences while working with other task groups. Tell others about your previous negative experiences rather than focusing on the task at hand.

READINGS

Clark, C. (1977). Grief Assessment and Intervention. In *Nursing concepts and processes*. Albany, NY: Delmar.

Clark, C. (1977). Learning to negotiate the system: A clinical experience in group dynamics. *Nursing Outlook 25* (1), 39–42.

Dinkmeyer, D. & Muro, J. (1971). *Group Counseling*. Itasca, IL: F.E. Peacock.

Dracup, K. et al. (1984). Group counseling in cardiac rehabilitation: Effect on patient compliance. *Patient Education and Counseling, 6* (4),169–177.

Duxbury, M. et al.(1984). Head nurse leadership Style with staff nurses burnout and job satisfaction in neonatal intensive care units. *Nursing Research 33* (2), 97–101.

Evans, R. et al. (1985). Cognitive therapy to achieve personal goals: Results of telephone group counseling with disabled adults. *Archives of Physical Medicine and Rehabilitation, 66* (10), 693–696.

Glasser, P., Sarri, R. & Vintner, R. (eds.) (1974). *Individual change through small groups*. New York: Macmillan.

Gray, R. (1974). Grief. *Nursing '74, 4,* 25–27.

Jacobsen-Webb, M. (1985). Increasing team skills: an evaluation of program effectiveness. *Journal of Allied Health 14* (4), 387–394.

Johnson, D. & Johnson, F. (1975). *Joining together: Group theory and group skills* (pp. 87–107). Englewood Cliffs, NJ: Prentice-Hall.

Lang, M. (1984). A way to manage job stress using a design-making model. *Journal of Continuing Education in Nursing 15* (3), 82–84.

Marram, G. (1973). *The group approach in nursing practice*. St. Louis, MO: Mosby.

Moynihan, R. et al. (1984). Nursing support groups in a cancer center. *Journal of Psychological Oncology 2* (1), 33–48.

Pothier, P. (1976). *Mental health counseling with children* (pp. 93–102). Boston: Little, Brown.

Ross, H. (1984). Working with groups on patient education. *Patient Education Counseling, 6* (3), 105–112.

Weisman, A. (1972). *On dying and denying*. New York: Behavioral Publications.

Youseff, F. (1984). Crisis intervention: A group therapy approach for hospitalized breast cancer patients. *Journal of Advanced Nursing 9* (3), 307–313.

6
Supervision of Group Leaders and Coleadership

SUPERVISION

In group work, supervision refers to the interpersonal process whereby leaders present specific data from group sessions to a supervisor in order to receive feedback about their leadership ability. Supervision of group leaders can occur in a number of different settings and in a variety of ways. Regardless of these variables, the group leader is always entirely responsible for what happens in the group. Although able to influence the group leader, the supervisor cannot be responsible for group process when not present in the group.

Group-work supervision can occur in individual or group settings. The novice group leader may meet individually with a nursing instructor, expert group leader, or fellow student to receive feedback about group leadership skills. This feedback is important because all people have "blind spots" in their perception that can operate to impede group movement, but of which they are unaware. Peers who are no more experienced than the group leader can often provide more objective perceptions because they have not yet been subjected to the pressures and stresses of the group. At the student level, peer supervision involves students supervising one another in their group work, under the guidance of an instructor. By serving as supervisors for one another, they learn not only how to be leaders, but also how to supervise others. Some questions the peer supervisor needs to ask when supervising other group leaders are:

Did the leader make assumptions without having sufficient data to support them?

Were theory or concepts regarding observations applied in an appropriate way?

Were recordings or presentations difficult to understand?

Were there noticeable gaps in presentation of observations or thoughts?

Were enough alternative leader actions suggested?

What evidences were there of transference and countertransference?

Was the peer supervisor critical or overbearing with the supervisee?

Did the peer supervisor create an open, comfortable environment for supervision?

What needs to be included in an evaluation of the supervisee that the peer supervisor will share with the nursing instructor or supervisor?

Figures 6-1 and 6-2 show the results of one hour of peer supervision from both the supervisor's and the supervisee's viewpoint.

Nursing students and graduate students in nursing who lead groups as part of their clinical experience usually receive supervision from nursing faculty. Written or verbal presentations of group process recordings are often used. In some instances, students present videotaped or audiotaped portions of a group session that is being supervised.

In whatever setting supervision occurs, it must focus partly on the supervisory process and on how it relates to group process. It is not unusual for the person being supervised to replicate struggles that are occurring in the group. For example, when the supervisee is competitive, reluctant, anxious, dependent, or angry, it is most likely that the

Supervisors: *S. C., J. B.*

Supervisees: *C. G., S. T.*

Date of Supervision: *12/11/87*

Type of Group: *Sensory Motor*

Supervision of *3rd group session*

Stimulation for 5-year-olds

5 minutes 1. Problems encountered with this session:

    a. *monopolizing by Teddy*

    b. *Tommy and Sue vie for leader's attention*

    c. *limited attention span of group*

    d. *high anxiety level of leader*

5 minutes 2. Themes:

    a. *competition,*
       e.g., all trying to be first

    b. *fantasy,*
       e.g., Tommy pretended the toys were real animals

5 minutes 3. Transferences and countertransferences:

    a. *Tommy looked at leader when crying;*
       Susie called him a baby;
       leader said (protectively),
       "He is not a baby!"
       (countertransference)

    b. *leader sees monopolizer*
       as a "smarty pants"
       (countertransference)

(continued)

FIGURE 6-1 Group peer supervisee form.

FIGURE 6-1 *(continued)*

---

      c. leader angry with group
         for "abandoning me"
         by leaving 5 minutes early
         (countertransference)

5 minutes   4.   Problems we want help with:

      a. recognizing transferences and
         countertransferences when
         they occur

      b. help in using facilitating questions

      c. drawing out the silent member

      d. adjusting to a new member

Evaluation of Supervisors' assistance:

1. Helped us to organize our presentation
   and told us when to move on to the next
   part of our presentation.

2. Pointed out our progress in recognizing
   transferences and countertransferences;
   suggested we go through our recordings
   to see what group events seem to evoke
   our under- or overreactions.

3. Explored reasons for silence of member;
   agreed new member was probably uncomfortable
   and would talk when ready.

---

4. Suggested facilitative questions, e.g.,
   "What are your thoughts?" rather than,
   "Do you agree?"

5. Asked questions when they needed more information;
   put us at ease by not confronting us or
   being negative.

6. Helped us to see how we were competing
   for the group's approval.

same struggles are occurring within the group led by that supervisee.

Because group leaders may feel quite unsure about their effectiveness as leaders, they may be hesitant to participate in the supervisory process. Presenting one's work to others is bound to create some anxiety in the group leader. Also, inexperienced group leaders may be alarmed to find that they have some of the same feelings about being in the group that other group members have. For example, the leader of a new group may feel just as anxious in the beginning as the group members do; or the leader may feel anger, sadness, or guilt that parallels group members' feelings when a group experience ends. Student group leaders often devalue their contributions to a group experience and may feel quite guilty and frustrated about their leadership accomplishments or their sense of relief that the experience is over. Anger, too, can be experienced by the group leader who feels that termination of the group also terminates a chance to learn and to experience satisfaction; these feelings of loss may be expressed as anger toward the group supervisor, school, or agency, who are viewed as depriving

Supervisors: *S.C., J.B.*   Supervisees: *C.G., S.T.*

Date of Supervision: *12/11/87*   Type of Group: *Sensory Motor*

Supervision of *3rd group session*   *Stimulation for 5-year-olds*

1. Problems supervisees encountered with this session

   monopolizing
   vying for leader's attention
   limited attention span
   high leader anxiety

2. Themes supervisees identified

   competition, fantasy

3. Themes identified through supervision

   competition between coleaders
   denial of group feeling

4. Transferences and countertransferences

   leader acted protectively toward Tommy
   (countertransference)
   Tommy looked to leader as parent (transference)
   leader angry with monopolizer
   ("smarty pants")
   leader angry with group for leaving early

5. Problems supervisees want assistance with

   recognizing transferences and
   countertransferences;
   using facilitating questions;
   drawing out silent member;
   new member

FIGURE 6-2 Group peer supervisor form.

6. Suggestions we made to supervisees:

go through process recordings for evidences
  of transferences and countertransferences
not to use questions that can be answered
  with a "yes" or "no"
that silent member may be anxious

7. Evaluation of supervisees' presentation:

Needed minimal direction in presenting data;
  presented clear, relevant information
  in all four areas.
Showed ability to question their behavior
  and listen to our ideas without using
  denial.
showed ability to apply group concepts and
  to identify group process.
We think they did an excellent job!

the student leader of a good learning experience. Because some of these feelings may be strong and uncomfortable, the novice group leader may try to avoid them, tending to censor data or to try to escape from exposure. It is important for group leaders to talk through their difficulties with a supervisor to lessen the potential for acting out their feelings in the group.

Graduate nurses often lead groups as part of their professional role. If nurses desire to further develop their group leadership skills, they need to obtain adequate clinical supervision, which should be supplied by the employing agency. If no expert group leader is available at the agency, the less experienced nurse leader can ask that the agency purchase supervision from a nursing group consultant or be paid for as part of a continuing education program. Or, the agency should provide funds and time for the nurse to obtain supervision on a private basis. Ongoing supervision is especially important when the nurse leads a supportive or therapeutic group; a brief course in group dynamics cannot provide the nurse with all the skills necessary to be a proficient leader.

Regardless of the level of skill or experience of a group leader, certain processes and leader signals point to the need for supervision. Leaders who answer in the affirmative to any of the following questions probably need supervision:

Do problems arise in beginning a new group?
Are tension or anxiety levels in the group high?
Is conflict that is not useful proliferating?
Is the group apathetic?
Is decision making unilateral or fragmented?
Is leadership autocratic?
Is the group lacking in cohesiveness?
Does the group continue in the orientation phase for more than six sessions?
Do one or more members always monopolize group sessions?
Is one group member being scapegoated?
Are silences usually broken by the leader?
Are new members about to enter the group?
Do group members leave the group abruptly?
Are members absent frequently?
Does physically aggressive behavior occur in the group?
Are group members primarily nonverbal?
Is the group approaching termination?
Does the group seem unable to reach its goals no matter what is tried?

Apart from group-process signals that point to a need for supervision, group leader signals may also indicate a need for assistance from an experienced group leader. Many social, educational, or work factors can make the leader more susceptible to group pressures and precipitate countertransference reactions in both the novice and in the experienced leader. One is the presence of reality events in the leader's life situation that may create added stress. Another is the leader's need to be successful or to be recognized as competent; when the group members show anger or frustration rather than expressing praise or appreciation, the leader may have countertransference reactions. Still another factor is a past significant relationship between the leader and the group, which can impair the leader's ability to see situations as the group sees it. Finally, countertransference reactions in the leader can result from the communication of individual or group anxiety to the leader; to prevent this, leaders need to know how to differentiate their own anxiety about the group from the anxiety transmitted by the group. Unless novice group leaders learn to deal with the countertransference response adequately, they may leave a group prematurely or feel guilty, disappointed, or frightened. For this reason, the beginning leader needs to take responsibility for seeking out adequate supervision. One way to do this is to share perceptions and reactions in classroom discussion with an advisor rather than discussing the exact sentence-by-sentence exchange that occurred in the group. Another way is to ask for individual appointment time with a more experienced group leader or to submit written or taped recordings and ask for assistance in analyzing the situation that brought the countertransference about.

Beginning group leaders may feel angry when their unrealistic goals for group movement are not met. Some leaders report overwhelming feelings of guilt, followed by irritation and eventual apathy when group members do not respond as the leaders had hoped they would. Sometimes the irritation and anger are forced underground, and the leader may end up being overprotective of group members or unable to stick firmly to limits for group behavior. One of the most frequent signs of countertransference is a feeling of physical illness or discomfort: diarrhea, muscular aches, headaches, or even persistent colds. Other important symptoms are an inability to focus on what is happening in the group, which can lead to a rejecting attitude toward group members, or other strong positive or negative feelings. Whatever the signs and symptoms, the group leader, especially the novice, who becomes aware that countertransference is occurring needs to seek out supervision.

COLEADERSHIP

The question of whether there should be one or two (or even multiple) leaders of a group is a moot point. Some leaders prefer to work with another person; others feel that working alone is best for them. Agency requirements may dictate coleadership. In some teaching institutions, it is common practice to pair a more experienced group leader with a novice. This arrangement provides the less experienced leader with a role model to imitate. In other institutions, two trainees are paired, in the hope that they will learn from each other.

Coleading a group with another person has advantages and disadvantages that need to be considered carefully prior to starting work with the group, because this type of leadership creates a more complex situation than individual leadership. In general, it is not recommended that leaders work in teams casually; the two leaders must be as seriously committed to working on the relationship between themselves as to working on that between themselves and the group members. In addition, the supervisory process must be relentlessly focused on the coleader relationship, since teams are particularly vulnerable to transference and countertransference reactions. Having two leaders gives the group an opportunity to try to play one leader off against the other, in much the same way as a child turns to father when mother denies a request.

Another difficulty of coleading a group is that the leader

who talks the most, the one who has the most group experience, or the one toward whom the group has the most positive transference feelings may end up being perceived as the senior leader, and the other will be seen as the junior person. This situation can create tension, because the group will be uncertain about the leaders' roles. The difficulty can sometimes be dealt with to some extent by having the coleaders interview prospective group members together.

Coleading can have disadvantages when efficient use of leaders is an important factor. The group size cannot be doubled just because another leader is added. Therefore, only half the number of groups can be run as when there is only one leader per group. Coleading is also not useful in a group with very young children, because they are often unable to relate to more than one adult at a time.

Lastly, any disagreement or strain between leaders is quickly sensed by the group. This situation is analogous to another family phenomenon wherein the children of fighting parents may react by trying to mediate, by feeling guilty because they think they may be the cause of the disagreement, by withdrawing as if trying to escape the situation, or by "acting up" to direct the parents' anger toward them instead of toward each other. Any of these group reactions can be counterproductive because members use their energy in trying to help the leaders instead of working at their task. Anxiety and inhibited group functioning may be an offshoot of leader disagreement. Trying to hide a disagreement will not be helpful either, because undercover disagreement can be as destructive as open disagreement, if not more so. At the same time, coleaders need to acknowledge the probability of some disagreement, since this occurs whenever two individuals attempt to form a relationship.

Although these disadvantages of coleadership are very real, ways can be found to decrease the potential for group movement to be hampered by them. In the first place, the coleaders should meet before the sessions begin for the sole purpose of becoming acquainted with each other as people.

Openness and respect should prevail. Each leader could draw up a list of questions to ask the other. There is bound to be some difference in their approaches to group interventions, but the differences should not be so great that the two cannot work together. The coleaders might discuss such questions as:

What are your goals for this group?
What is your theoretical orientation to group leading?
How do you see yourself functioning in this group?
How do you see me functioning in this group?
What group-leader strengths do you think you have?
What group-leader weaknesses do you think you have?
What suggestions do you have for handling possible disagreements between us in the group?
Do you think we will try to compete with each other and, if so, how can we recognize and deal with this to keep it from interfering with group movement?
How do you feel about our seeking out supervision?
How could we present group data to a supervisor?
What are your thoughts about how we can deal with such group problems as monopolizing, scapegoating, silence, new members, transferences, physical aggression, nonverbal members, absences, and manipulation?

One or more meetings prior to the beginning of the coleadership experience can decrease the likelihood that each coleader will try to meet his or her own needs rather than the needs of the group. If the coleaders wish to continue to monitor their activities in the group, they could meet together after each session to review group process, validate one another's perceptions of group events, identify special needs of the group, and identify areas of growth and the need for supervision of the coleaders. Ideally, some of these postmeeting sessions should include a more experienced group leader.

One purpose of the postmeeting session is to give the

leaders a chance to deal with any disagreement they may have about how to handle the group process. During the orientation phase it is not wise to attempt to try to settle any disagreement within the group context, since the focus at this stage of group development is on the establishment of a sense of trust in the leaders. Many coleaders continue to deal with any disagreements outside of the group even later in the group process. This approach is reminiscent of that taken by parents who discuss problems in their relationship when children are not present. On the other hand, some coleaders have begun to think that if their disagreements can take place within the group, in an atmosphere of trust and respect, they can teach group members how to disagree yet continue to work together effectively. If the leaders can manage this, the group could have powerful learning experiences in effective interpersonal relationships. However, this approach should be used with caution. It should not be attempted unless the coleaders have worked through their relationship so as to be able to disagree without becoming angry; in most cases this requires supervision and practice.

Coleading does offer several advantages over single leadership:

1. Novice group leaders can observe a more experienced leader in action, and they can gradually assume leadership functions as they become comfortable in those roles. Moving from a more structured, dependent role to a less structured, interdependent role can provide support and decrease the anxiety level of the beginning leader.

2. Inexperienced leaders who work with more experienced group observers have an opportunity to validate their perceptions of group process.

3. Coleaders can act as role models for the group by demonstrating how to communicate clearly, cooperate, collaborate, and disagree effectively.

4. The coleadership relationship re-creates the family situation of mother and father; such a re-creation can be

especially useful when working with parents, families, or children. Regardless of the leaders' sex, they can be perceived as parental figures by group members, thus making transference reactions clearer and more easily identifiable.

5. Coleaders can act in complementary roles, each reenforcing the other. For example, one can act as nonverbal observer of group process for one session, while the other is verbal and directs group interaction. The nurse who acts as nonverbal observer may also serve as recorder for that session. In postmeeting sessions, the observer/recorder can give the coleader helpful feedback on group process. For the next session, the two may reverse these roles, or not. In the latter case, there is less need to work out the relationship within the group, but time is required to work out how continuity will be maintained when leaders do alternate roles. Even though the pair may seem to be working as a single leader, there is still a tendency to compete with one another as leaders, to compare one's leading style with one's partners, and to disagree about how to approach group problems. It is not unusual for group members to try to create a division between the group leaders by complimenting that day's leader, by complaining about last week's leader, or by acting in ways divisive to the leadership pair. For these reasons, postmeeting sessions can be helpful even in a complementary role arrangement.

Another way a pair of leaders can work together in a group is for one leader to focus on the group process, while the other focuses on individual members. This approach can be especially effective with individual group members who may need more structured situations. In such cases, one leader can move around the group, orienting confused group members to group events, providing physical and emotional support by sitting next to anxious or disruptive group members, and by setting limits on disruptive behavior. A final advantage of the coleadership situation is that it allows the group to continue during the absence of one of the leaders.

SIMULATED EXERCISES

Each of the two simulated exercises that follow includes an experiential and a discussion section. If either exercise is completed without an instructor or supervisor present, participants should plan to share difficulties and insights with a more experienced group leader following the completion of the exercises.

EXERCISE 1 Assertive Behavior

This skill exercise can be used whenever participants find it difficult to state their wishes, desires, or needs in an assertive way. Peer supervision is a component of this exercise.

The exercise helps to develop skill in "I" assertive presentations of self. Withdrawal and/or "You" aggressive responses are replaced by clear, consistent messages.

Each person is to identify one situation where she wishes she had been able to say, "This is what I think," "This is what I feel," or "This is what I want."

Objectives
1. To identify interpersonal situations in which aggressive or withdrawal behavior was used.
2. To practice giving "I" assertive messages.
3. To practice giving feedback to others about their communication.

Procedure

1. The group or the instructor appoints a timekeeper, who makes sure that agreed-upon time limits for each step are observed. The timekeeper is also responsible for warning the group when five minutes are left to accomplish the task.

10–15 minutes
2. The larger group breaks into pairs. One person in the pair briefs the other on the situation from which she withdrew or became aggressive instead of assertive. The first person then practices saying, in an assertive manner, whatever was not said in the actual situation. The second gives feedback to help bring out assertiveness: "Look me in the eye when you say that," or "Don't laugh when you say that," or "Your words say one thing but your face says another."

10–15 minutes
3. The leader asks the pairs to reverse roles and the second person in the pair briefs the other person on the situation in which she was unable to be assertive. The pairs then proceed as described in number 2 above.

15–30 minutes
4. The entire group reconvenes and discusses the simulations, focusing on the following points:
   a. How did it feel to be assertive?
   b. What prevented each person from being assertive in the original situation? Were their fears realistic?
   c. What was learned from this exercise that can be applied in other situations?

EXERCISE 2 Peer Supervision

This exercise is useful for developing skills as peer supervisor and peer supervisee.

Objectives
1. To learn to use supervisory time efficiently by focusing on the issues of themes, transferences, countertransferences, problems encountered in the group, and problems that cannot be solved without assistance.
2. To practice presenting group-process data verbally.
3. To practice commenting on others' data presentations in a non-threatening way.

Procedure

1. The larger group breaks into subgroups of five; two will have the role of supervisor, two will be supervisees, and one will be timekeeper.

2. Each subgroup appoints one of its members to be the timekeeper, who is responsible for making sure that the supervisees present data for no more than 20 minutes.

3. The supervisees (or coleaders) are directed by the timekeeper to begin presenting data to the group, but first to look at the guide on page 158 of this book. Meanwhile, the timekeeper briefs the other two group members on their roles as supervisors.

5–30 minutes
4. The timekeeper tells the supervisors to follow the guide on page 158 when taking notes on the supervisee(s) presentation. The supervisors are to ensure that all four areas are covered during the 20-minute presentation period. If supervisees spend too much or too little time on any area, the supervisors (coached by the timekeeper) are to redirect the presentation with comments such as: "Let's move on to countertransferences now," "What about themes?" or "Tell us some more about the problems in the group that we might be able to help you with."

20 minutes
5. When both supervisee(s) and supervisors are ready to begin, the timekeeper begins timing the presentation, warns the group when only five minutes of presentation time remain, and calls time when 20 minutes have elapsed.

20 minutes
6. Supervisors criticize the supervisee(s)' presentation, give suggestions for handling group problems, point out omissions in data, and compliment the presenter(s) on strengths.

(continued)

EXERCISE 2 (*continued*)

10–30   7. Each member of the group is asked by the timekeeper to
minutes   tell what was learned from this experience and in what
             ways peer supervisors or supervisees could have been
             more effective in their roles.

Peer Group Supervision Presentation Guide

You have 20 minutes to present data about one or more group sessions
you have led. Be sure to cover all four areas below in the alloted time
period.

Group themes

Group problems (monopolizing, scapegoating, anxiety, conflict, decision
         making, and so on)

Transferences and countertransferences

Problems the leader(s) need help with

READINGS

Allen, J. (1975). Peer group supervision in family therapy. *Child Welfare 55*, 423–439.

Armony, N. (1975). Countertransference: Obstacle and Instrument. *Contemporary Psychoanalysis 11*, 265–281.

Aroskar, M. (1985). Nurses as decision makers: Ethical dimensions. *Imprint 32* (4), 28–31.

Burnside, I. (1971). Peer supervision: A method of teaching. *Journal of Nursing Education 10*, 15–22.

Clark, D. (1972). A social systems approach to short-term psychiatric care. *Perspectives in Psychiatric Care 10,* 178–182.

Cooper, L. et al. (1985). Supervision in a group: An application of group theory. *Clinical Supervision 3* (2), 7–25.

Fensterheim, H. & Baer, J. (1975). *Don't say yes when you want to say no.* New York: Dell.

Fuchs, L. (1975). Reflections on touching and transference in psychotherapy. *Clinical Social Work Journal 3*, 167–176.

Kabcenell, R. (1974). On countertransference. *Psychoanalytic Study of the Child 29*, 27–33.

Lane, R. (1974). The influence of supervision on trainee's development of facilitative skills in counseling. *Dissertation Abstracts International 34*, 4748–4749.

Morrow, R. (1975). Symposium: ethnic differences in therapeutic relationships. *Professional Psychology 6*, 468–469.

Munn, H. (1985). Assessing supervisory leadership behavior. *Health Care Supervisor 4* (1), 1–13.

Munson, C. (1983). Supervision of co-therapist conflict. *Clinical Supervision 1* (4), 63–76.

Semmelroth, C. & Semmelroth S. (1975). The need for better supervision among mental health professionals. *Improving Human Performance Quarterly 4*, 37–42.

Smith, M. (1975). *When I say no, I feel guilty.* New York: Dial.

Taubman, B. (1976). *How To Become an Assertive Woman.* New York: Pocket Books.

Termini, M. & Hauser, M. (1973). The process of the supervisory relationship. *Perspectives in Psychiatric Care 11*, 121–125.

7
Behavioral Approaches for Group Leaders

The term "behavioral modification" or "the behavioral approach" refers to an approach that focuses on behavioral change and is based on certain principles of learning, such as reinforcement. To some extent, all communication can be said to be behaviorally oriented, since it usually represents an attempt to influence others. The leader who nods in approval when a group member speaks reinforces that behavior, thus increasing the possibility that it will occur more frequently. The behavioral approach is not concerned with insight or with whether the person understands why he acts as he does, but it focuses on decreasing unsatisfying or disruptive behavior and on increasing satisfying, goal-directed behavior.

A behavioral approach considers the individual's present difficulties, identifies specific behaviors that must be changed, counts the frequency of each behavior (baseline data), and then uses reinforcement to increase desired behaviors. The behavioral approach can be used in a number of ways in a group setting. One way is to gather together a group of either staff members or clients in order to teach them assertive behavior. Behavioral modification techniques can also be used to help one or more group members to make more verbal statements, or to decrease disruptive behavior in others. Yet another way to use this approach is to gather together parents who are concerned about their children's behavior. Common behavioral patterns that can be dealt with by teaching parents certain behavioral approaches include complaining, soiling, teasing, truancy, temper tantrums, sulking, not picking up toys or possessions, and crying.

ASSERTIVENESS

An *assertive* person demonstrates through words and actions that "This is what I think. This is what I feel. This is what I want." Assertive people set goals, act on achieved goals in a clear and consistent way, and take responsibility for the consequences of those actions. In contrast, *aggressive* behavior has a controlling or manipulating aspect that is often hidden, out of proportion to the relationships, or off the point of discussion. In assertive behavior, a person states and stands up for his rights, knowing full well that others may disagree or attempt to block his action. The assertive person gives clear and open messages about what is desired.

Giving "I" Messages

The first way a leader can help a group to become less aggressive or withdrawn and more assertive is to teach the members to give "I" messages. Such messages convey how the individual thinks or feels: "I can't help you now." "I don't like to be shouted at." "I believe your figures are wrong." "I want to talk this over with you." "I feel angry." "I feel guilty about being late." "I feel uncomfortable." "(I) thank you." "I disagree with that." These "I"-assertive messages are definitely different from "you"-aggressive messages that place blame on the other person, who then tends to become defensive: "You know I'm busy." "Don't you shout at me!" "Can't you ever add this up right?" "You don't know what you're talking about!" "Stop meddling in my work." "Why do you always start the group so early?" "Why are you always picking on me?" When increasing assertiveness is a goal, the leader should stop any member who gives a "You" message during a session and ask him to restate it in "I"-message form.

CHANGING UNWANTED HABITS

An experienced group leader can teach group members how to identify and change unwanted habits. Five steps are involved in developing this skill.

The first step is to express the habit in behaviors that can be counted or measured. For example, if the objective is to increase one's ability to communicate effectively with coworkers, one could count frequency of direct eye contact, loudness and firmness of the speaking voice, and whether the speaker sticks to the point or makes qualifying statements—"I'm sorry, but . . ." or "This is probably not right, but. . . ."

The next step is to count the selected behaviors over at least a week's time. This data will give the person a baseline to use in checking progress in changing the habit.

The third step is to determine what precedes the unwanted habit behavior. For example, does the person have difficulty only when speaking with coworkers in a group setting, or only when speaking to a certain coworker? Is there a beginning or midpoint at which the habitual behavior could be interrupted? At what point does it seem impossible to interrupt the habitual behavior?

The fourth step is to have the individual make a contract of intention to change the habit. In this case, group members can make contracts with other group members. Contracts may be verbal or written, but they should contain simple, attainable goals. A reasonable beginning contract might be: "I will look directly into the group leader's eyes when speaking to her." Once the objective of this contract has been met for several sessions, it can be expanded to include looking into all group members' eyes when speaking to them. Each time a contract is fulfilled, the next contract can be aimed at correcting more difficult behaviors. When all the group members' counted behaviors have been changed, the leader can set up role-playing situations in which group members describe a coworker with whom they have been unable to communicate directly. Practice sessions using tape recordings and/or videotape can give group members feedback about how well they communicate with others. The group members can then practice communicating directly with one person playing the coworker role. Finally, the contract can be extended to include extragroup behaviors with the real coworker.

The final step in the process is to try to arrange the environmental elements so that the goal will be easy to reach. For example, approaching coworkers for discussions might be most fruitful when all concerned are neither rushed nor fatigued.

INCREASING COOPERATIVE BEHAVIORS

Group members who are unusually noisy, inattentive, or nonverbal are prime candidates for taking on the scapegoat role. As soon as the leader notices that a group member does not sit still, leaves the group, loudly interrupts others, or does not speak clearly, this should be a signal to begin to plan an intervention, perhaps using the behavioral approach.

In this approach, the leader's first task is to differentiate between behaviors that are deviative and those that are cooperative. For example, some deviating behaviors in a group might be getting out of one's chair, interrupting while another person is talking, and not answering when asked a question.

The second task is to record *baseline data*. This kind of data gives the answers to several questions. How often during a certain time unit does the group member get out of his chair? How often per time unit does he interrupt another person? How often per time unit does he fail to answer when asked a question? Several group sessions will probably be needed to establish the average frequency of each behavior. These baseline data need not be kept a secret. In fact, people are sometimes influenced to change their behavior just by knowing how frequently a certain action occurs. The noncooperative member or other group members can be enlisted in this data-collecting procedure, depending on the leader's judgment.

The next step is to pinpoint the events that precede the unwanted behaviors being studied. Often the leader or other group members may be instrumental in setting off noncooperative behavior. For example, the leader may reinforce a group member's disruptive comment by paying undue attention to it; this is often a signal for the member to continue being disruptive. It may be assumed that there are some current rewarding consequences of the behavior. The leader might formulate several functional hypotheses regarding what particular reinforcement is maintaining the noncooperative behavior and then test these out through observation and experimentation. Although the leader may have hunches about what the member finds rewarding in noncooperative behavior, it is imperative that such rewards should not be removed during the baseline data-gathering period.

Many reinforcers—a smile, a nod, or a grimace—would seem to have low influence, yet they can maintain a group member's behavior. The leader's task as interventionist is to alter the milieu so that the most powerful reinforcers will be those that strengthen cooperative behavior.

One way to find out what is reinforcing or rewarding to a group member may be to ask; during or after a group session, the leader might ask some or all of the following questions: "What do you like to do best?" "What would make it more pleasant for you in the group?" "Which person in the group do you feel most comfortable with?" If the group member can answer any or all of these questions, the leader can then begin to formulate ideas about how to elicit cooperative behavior from him. For example, if a group member says that getting up from the chair relieves tension, the leader might contract to exchange 1 minute of getting up after each question answered with three or more words. This contract may be verbal or written. In carrying out the contract, the leader may involve the group in giving support to cooperative behavior by saying, "We have a group problem to help Tom learn how to answer questions more effectively. I've devised a plan that may work. Wendy, will you keep track of the number of words, make sure he gets to take his prize of being out of his chair for one minute." When it is difficult to engage the group in assisting with the contract, the leader could try the *token system,* in which members who volunteer to assist with the contract may earn tokens or other privileges. The leader decides whether or not the tokens can be turned in later for more concrete rewards, such as candy, cake, a group termination party, or some other reward decided on by the group.

When working with a group of children or adolescents, the leader can ask parents to provide reinforcers. Allowances, television viewing, or other special privileges can be granted by the parents when they receive a note or call from the leader indicating that a reward has been earned. When working with others in providing rewards, the leader needs to structure the relationship so that whoever else is involved also gets rewarded for being consistent in dispensing rewards. If this facet is not considered, parents or others will not be motivated to collaborate.

Whether a contract is written or verbal, it may be to the leader's advantage to enlist the support of other group members in helping the noncooperative member count words spoken and remind the member to get out of his chair. Thus other group members are cast in the role of helping, supportive, and cooperative persons, and they are less likely to scapegoat the noncooperative member because they will be rewarded by the group leader's comments and praise for their efforts.

Another way to involve all group members in the contract is to use charts or graphs to show progress toward the goal. Stars, checks, or other measures of progress can be used by the leader or by other group members to demonstrate and reinforce concrete movement toward a goal. The leader may wish to comment to the group on a member's progress as a further reward for movement toward more appropriate behavior.

Involving the group as reinforcers will only work when several factors have been considered. First, the group must be able to dispense the reinforcers. If the noncooperative member says that the only pleasant thing is a hot fudge sundae, and he is on a diabetic diet, the reinforcer cannot be dispensed. Then, the group may have to search for other reinforcers by observing what pleases him, or by asking family members or friends what pleases him. Second, the reinforcer can only be given as stated in the contract. Also, the reward must be given each time the cooperative behavior occurs, without exception, since it is the consistency of the reinforcing response that will maintain the cooperative behavior. Additional reinforcers may also develop in time; for example, other group members will probably become more friendly toward him, and this new reinforcer will help to maintain the cooperative behavior. A third factor that needs to be considered is the way the leader presents the contract. It must be presented in a matter-of-fact, nonpunitive style, with no verbal or nonverbal comments about noncooperative behavior, since the purpose of the contract is to reward cooperative behavior. The leader concentrates on changing one behavior before moving on to the next target behavior. For this reason, the most disturbing behavior is dealt with first. In the example given above, the getting-out-of-seat behavior may decrease simply due to satiation; that is, the group member may be able to get out of his seat—and in fact is encouraged to do so—whenever he wishes to answer with three words or more. At a certain point, getting out of his chair may become more of a task than a reward. Once other group members start reinforcing his verbalizations, he may learn that talking can be more pleasurable than leaving the group circle.

In addition to using reinforcers to promote wanted behaviors, the group leader can use behavioral modification techniques to help members develop new behaviors. One such technique is called shaping. *Shaping* is the reinforcement of successive approximations toward the desired behavior. For example, if the goal is to get one member to talk to another group member, the first desirable behavior may be to look at that person. By praising or rewarding the member for first looking at another group member, the leader can shape behavior in the desired direction. Other desirable behaviors, such as maintaining eye contact and saying hello to the other, would also be praised. The idea of shaping is that each small step toward the goal is praised, and thus the group member slowly develops the entire repertoire needed to achieve the goal in the end.

A second behavioral modification technique is *prompting*. The leader tells the group member how to perform one or more steps in the desired behavior pattern. For example: "Look at Sally now; look right in her eyes and say hello." The techniques of prompting and shaping are frequently combined to achieve an appropriate response.

Modeling is another useful behavioral modification technique. In modeling, the leader demonstrates the desired behaviors. For example, the leader might say, "Watch me as I talk with Karen." Modeling can also be used more indirectly. Group members naturally imitate significant other people; thus, as a significant person in the group, the leader models behavior whenever she teaches the group how to interact by interacting with them. The leader might also use as role models group members who are proficient in a skill.

Another behavioral modification technique is the use of *incompatible responses*. This can be used when the desired behavior is incompatible with the undesired behavior. For example, the undesired behavior in a teaching group may be classroom disruption. Therefore, the target behavior may be academic performance. The rationale for choosing to focus on academic performance is that adequate performance in this area is incompatible with classroom disruption. The initial behavior required to be eligible for a reward should be easily attainable. A beginning behavior might be to open a book or to hold learning materials. Once the disruptive member has attained this goal, a more complex goal, such as reading two paragraphs of the book or learning the purpose of one piece of equipment, will be sufficient to receive the reward. Gradually, the level of accomplishment is raised to include understanding of more complex learning material.

WORKING WITH PARENTS

Until recently, parenting was thought of as an innate skill. Now it seems an accepted fact that people do need assistance in learning to be effective parents. The group setting can be an especially productive environment for learning parenting skills, since parents can learn from one another as well as from the leader.

Some skills parents can learn in group sessions are how to praise and give reinforcers for appropriate behavior, how to ignore deviant or inappropriate behavior, and how to implement three-minute "time-out" periods. The time-out period may consist of having the child go to his room to be alone for the time specified, or removing him from a pleasurable situation such as watching television or playing with his toys.

A group of parents can be taught how to specify behaviors, collect baseline data, select reinforcers, and develop contracts. While group members are collecting data at home, one or more of the problem behaviors can be selected by the leader for the group to explore. Parents whose children do not have that specific behavioral problem can model what they would do to handle the problem. The rest of the group can give feedback to the modeling parents, ask questions, and discuss their own difficulties in handling that problem.

Subsequent group sessions might be used to discuss difficulties and successes in using various behavioral approaches in the actual parenting situation. The leader will probably also have to deal with family resistance to certain behavioral modification methods. Such resistance is most likely to occur when parental discord and family disorganization is ongoing and chronic. In these instances, parents habitually provide inconsistent and contradictory cues to their children. When the leader notes that this is the case, the family can be referred for marital-pair psychotherapy, a type of therapy that deals with basic parental conflict. Another source of resistance occurs when parents insist that all children should be treated alike, without favoritism. Although parents frequently claim to practice nonfavoritism, they often individualize punishment. In such cases, the leader can try to extend behavioral modification techniques to include all the children. Another family resistance is related to the "needed family scapegoat" phenomenon. Here, the child's problem behavior serves a highly complex purpose in the family; as a result, when the behavior of this sibling improves, forms of disturbance or friction may appear in other family members. In such instances, parents should be referred to a family therapist. A nearly universal resistance to behavioral modification is the philosophy of not wanting to control another person's life. Parents frequently wish to be friends with their children, or at least hope to be viewed as permissive, progressive parents, and the group leader may need to present oral or written material about how parents reward and punish behavior in any case. What the behavioral approach teaches is how to reward positive behavior consistently and effectively.

SIMULATED EXERCISES

Two simulated exercises follow. Both are skill exercises, and for each a list of discussion questions is given. If the group is larger than 15, it should be divided into equal-size subgroups. When an experienced group leader is not present during the discussion session, a postexercise session should be held with a supervisor or instructor to discuss difficulties encountered.

EXERCISE 1   Preparing for Changes

This skill exercise can be used whenever a change such as termination, entrance of a new group member, or movement from one group phase to another is anticipated. It can also be used to increase flexibility to unknown change situations, since a problem-solving approach is taught.

The purpose of the exercise is to gain skill in planning for change, whether it is an anticipated or an unanticipated change. Changes are examined using a problem-solving approach that can be transferred to real-life situations.

Objectives
1. To learn a problem-solving approach to change.
2. To practice preparing for upcoming changes.

Procedure

1. The group appoints a timekeeper, who makes sure that time limits for each step are observed. Together, the group decides on what time limits will be used. The timekeeper orients the group at each step regarding how much time remains for the task.

2. The group or the instructor appoints a leader for each group.

10 minutes
3. The leader asks each group member to write down on a piece of paper a real or hypothetical change, what is to be learned from the change, what is to be produced as a result of the change, and what would be a reward or satisfaction as a result of the change.

30–60 minutes
4. The leader asks each group member in turn to tell the other group members what the change is, what is to be learned or produced, and what reward would be helpful. The leader then asks the group member what barriers there are to reaching the goal, what alternatives the person has, what resources are available, and what further planning for change is needed. If the group member is unable to answer any or all of these questions, the leader can ask, "Who in the group has a suggestion for this?"

15–45 minutes
5. The leader assists the group to discuss the following points:
   a. What is difficult about change?
   b. What could be rewarding about change?
   c. Is change seen by the majority of group members as satisfying? If no, why not? If yes, what opinions does the group have about this?

(continued)

EXERCISE 1 (*continued*)

d. What barriers seem to be mentioned most by group members? What ideas does the group have about why these barriers are mentioned most often? What can be done to remove barriers to change?

e. What seems to prevent group members from stating alternative actions or from identifying untapped resources?

f. What was learned from this exercise that can be applied in other situations?

EXERCISE 2 Teaching

This exercise can be used whenever the nurse leader requires skill in teaching others. The purpose of the exercise is to help the leader gain skill in preparing and delivering information to others. Skill in giving feedback to others' teaching efforts is also enhanced.

This exercise requires a great deal of preparation. Prior to undertaking it, each group member must be familiar with the content of the material to be taught and must have thought about presenting a 5-minute segment of the material to the group. Source materials, as well as the readings section at the end of this chapter and other chapters, may be consulted.

Objectives
1. To identify a topic suitable to be taught in the group format.
2. To list factors that need to be considered when teaching others.
3. To practice teaching in a group format.
4. To give and receive feedback on teaching skills.

Procedure

1. The group or instructor appoints a leader for each group.

75 minutes maximum

2. The leader asks each group member in turn to "teach" the rest of the group. The leader does not intervene in each person's teaching but allows it to go on for 5 minutes and then asks the group for helpful hints on teaching the content chosen. The leader also asks the group for feedback to the group member who taught on the following: What are important things to consider in teaching a group this material? What types of resources need to be considered? Does the teacher need to do further research on the content of her presentation? What principles of learning need to be considered further? What problems seem to be inherent in this teaching situation?

20–60 minutes

3. When every group member has finished presenting and received feedback, the leader assists the group to discuss the following questions:
   a. How does readiness affect learning?
   b. How can the teacher find out what the learner already knows?
   c. How does the teacher assess whether the presentation is too technical, complex, fast, or slow for the learner?
   d. How can anxiety affect learning? What can the leader or teacher do to decrease anxiety in the group?

(continued)

EXERCISE 2 (*continued*)

---

e. How can repetition and feedback be built into a teaching program?

f. What kind of media and equipment could be used to teach the material most effectively?

g. How can the teacher assist group members to share information with one another and participate in the teaching-learning experience?

h. What was learned from this exercise that can be applied in other situations?

READINGS

Bergnan, P. (1985). The use of assertiveness training in the clinical environment. *Journal of Nursing Education 24* (1), 33–35.

Berni, R. & Fordyce, W. (1973). Behavior modification and the nursing process. St. Louis, MO: Mosby.

Clark, C. (1977). Learning Through Teaching. In *Nursing concepts and processes*. Albany, NY: Delmar.

Fensterheim, H. & Baer, J. (1975). *Don't say yes when you want to say no*. New York: Dell.

Gordon, T. (1970). *Parent effectiveness training*. New York: New American Library.

Koerner, M. et al. (1985). Communicating in the OR: confrontation. Part 3. *Association of Operating Room Nurses 42* (2), 244–245, 247, 250–251.

Krumboltz, J. and Krumboltz, H. (1972). *Changing children's behavior*. Englewood Cliffs, NJ: Prentice-Hall.

Laird, M. (1975). Techniques for teaching pre- and postoperative patients. *American Journal of Nursing 75,* 1338–1340.

LeBow, M. (1976). *Approaches to modifying patient behavior*. New York: Appleton-Century-Crofts.

Loomis, M. & Horsley, J. (1974). *Interpersonal change: A behavioral approach to nursing practice*. New York: McGraw-Hill.

Mash, Eric, Handy, L. & Hanerlynck, L. (eds.) (1976). *Behavior modification approaches to parenting*. New York: Brunner/Mazel.

Pratt, S. & Fischer, J. (1975). Behavior modification: Changing hyperactive behavior in a children's group. *Perspectives in Psychiatric Care 12,* 37–42.

Ross, H. (1984). Working with groups in patient education. *Patient Education and Counseling 6* (3), 105–112.

Salzer, J. (1975). Classes to improve diabetic self-care. *American Journal of Nursing 75,* 1342–1326.

Schwab, M. et al. (1985). Relieving the anxiety and fear in dementia . . . music, exercise, touch, and relaxation administered in a group setting. *Journal of Gerontological Nursing 11* (5), 8–11, 14–15.

Smyth, K. (ed.). (1970). Symposium on patient teaching. *Nursing Clinics of North America 6,* 571–806.

Tharp, R. & Wetzel, R. (1969). *Behavior modification in the natural environment*. New York: Academic Press.

8
Recording

RECORDING IS IMPORTANT

Recording group interactions for study is important for a number of reasons. First, recording the multitude of verbal and nonverbal communications as they occur in a group meeting decreases the chances of omitting important details, since recall of events decreases rapidly with time. Second, recording what happens in the group will allow the group leader to review what happened within and across group sessions. Third, recording group interactions will help the leader to review group skills, to compare them with those previously demonstrated at other sessions, and to evaluate progress as a group leader. Fourth, recording will encourage the leader to think of what has been said or done in various group interactions, and this will increase the potential for dealing more effectively with similar situations in the future.

RECORDING METHODS

A number of methods can be utilized for recording group interactions for later study. Three of the most useful types of records are the written record, audiotape recordings, and videotape recordings.

Some group participants may become anxious when they

learn that a permanent record is being made of their behavior. The group recorder can usually prevent or decrease such anxiety among group members by:

1. Stating in a positive manner that recordings will be made. (e.g., "I'd like to record what happens in this group so I can learn about how groups work. (Pause.) Any comments?" or, "I'm going to be recording this meeting so I can learn how to be of more help to all of you. Any reactions to this?")

2. Telling the group members with whom the recording will be shared. (e.g., "I will share the recordings with my instructor and fellow students only," or, "The only people who will hear this tape are my supervisor and your social worker.")

3. Playing back a segment of the tape or showing the written notes to participants who seem especially anxious about the recording. This can be done at the end of a meeting or at the time of establishing that recordings will be done, depending on the insistence of the group members. Much anxiety about recordings seems to be related to how participants sound on tape or to the idea that the recorder is recording more than what is actually happening. Once participants hear how they sound on tape and/or what is being recorded, anxiety is minimized.

If none of these techniques works, the group leader is forced either to change the method of recording to one that is more acceptable to the group, or to stop recording. But before doing either of these things, the recorder can inquire, "What is it about recording that you object to?" Sometimes a group member will voice an objection, such as concern about confidentiality, that can be dealt with without stopping the recording. Generally, the group recorder will receive group consensus to record; rarely, if ever, do groups refuse to allow recording if the suggestions given here are followed.

Written Records

To be of most use later, the written record should be made at the time the group meets. Depending on the type of group interaction, the nurse who is recording the information needs to spend some time receiving group consent for this. In committee meetings, where a secretary usually takes notes in any case, there may be little difficulty in receiving group consent. But in supportive groups where members may fear disclosure of their comments it may be more difficult to get their consent to make a written record of the group session.

Once it has been decided that written records will be made, the nurse may need to practice recording before the group sessions actually begin. Experience in this skill can be gained through practice in simulated group situations. To be proficient in recording group interaction, several skills will have to be learned: a coding or symbol system for words or actions that occur frequently, a way to determine what is important to record and what is not, and the ability to observe and write at the same time. Novices at recording often complain of feeling overwhelmed ("There's too much to record"), or they worry that they are unable to tell what is important and what is not important to record ("I can't write down every sigh and frown; how do I know what to record?").

The nurse leader can develop a coding or symbol system for group interaction. For example, group members can be assigned numbers or initials, anxiety can be represented by a *, or silence by S. Common symbols used in nursing, such as c̄ for with, s̄ for without, can also be adopted to conserve time and space. Two advantages of the written record method are that little equipment is needed and that tapes need not be replayed after the group meeting in order to evaluate group interaction. Writing in a group may also be less intrusive and more acceptable to group members than would audio- or videotaping. A disadvantage of the written record is that nonverbal messages, such as body posture, eye contact, and gestures, may not be noted if the nurse becomes too involved in recording verbal communication. Usually, the nurse is unable to be a vocal group participant as well, since participating and recording are each a full-time function. This can be remedied by having two recorders: verbal and nonverbal.

Audiotape Records

Audiotape recording must be done while the group is in session. It is important for the leader to be familiar with the use of the audiotape equipment before the group meets. Audiovisual, educational technology, or library and learning resources technicians can be approached for assistance in this area. The meeting room should be checked out to make sure it is suitable for recording; in very noisy settings, unwanted sounds may be picked up which can override spoken conversation. The group recorder also has to place the microphone so that it will most effectively pick up all group members' remarks.

Some advantages of audiotaping are that the group recorder is free to join in the group discussion and can then evaluate leadership skills by listening to the tape at a later date, and that portions can be replayed to teach participants or to refresh memories about what really was said. (Hearing one's own voice make a statement is much less likely to be dismissed than hearing someone read back what was apparently said.) A major disadvantage of the audiotape method is that visual cues, such as gestures or movements, are not available for study. Therefore, the leader may wish to jot down important visual cues for later study. Another disadvantage is that it takes at least twice as long to listen to and evaluate a tape as it does to record the session. However, if the group recorder, instructor, and/or group supervisor is interested in hearing a tape rather than reading a written record, the audiotape may be the method of choice.

Videotape Records

Videotape equipment is used while the group is in session. Becoming proficient in the use of lights, cameras, and other needed equipment is mandatory and may become quite time-consuming. Consequently, the leader may need at first to request the assistance of a videotape technician or an experienced student. Lighting, noise/quietness, space, and other aspects of the environment must be adequately checked out before taping begins.

Some advantages of the videotape are that the group recorder is free to join the session, and a complete record of verbal and nonverbal communication is recorded, exactly as it occurred. Another major advantage of the videotape method is that portions can be played back to the group to demonstrate concepts, to review what was said, or to do on-the-spot teaching of participants. Disadvantages of videotape are that equipment is relatively heavy and unwieldy and not always available, and that, because of the intrusiveness of the method, it may take longer for group members to relax and participate in the group discussion.

THE GROUP RECORDING GUIDE

The Group Recording Guide, which has been tested with more than 100 beginning nurse leaders, was developed as a means of enhancing the leader's observation and leadership skills and recording ability. It tests for all the types of information a group recorder, observer, or leader needs in order to assess group interaction.

Supplementary Data Needed for Meaningful Recording

The top half of Figure 8-1 illustrates the type of supplementary data the leader needs to collect at the beginning of each recording session, before the actual discussion begins. (This part of the form is not repeated on succeeding pages of a single recording.) Seating arrangement may be highly

Seating Arrangement*:

Date: *February 6, 1987*

(R): *Leila J.*

(L): *Rose T.*

Type and purpose of group:

Reality orientation for nursing home residents

Group Recording Guide

Events	Analysis of Events	Leader Action	Evaluation of Leader Actions	Alternative Actions

*L = leader, R = recorder, ● = empty chairs.

FIGURE 8-1 Group recording guide.

significant, because it can reveal information about that session as well as offer comparison with other sessions. For example, if member number 1 always sits next to the leader, looks to the leader for answers to questions, and never initiates topics for discussion, the leader may well speculate that this member is highly dependent on her. Or if the leader and group recorder always sit next to one another and group members always leave an empty chair between themselves and the "authority figures" (L and R), the nurse may suspect that the group is not one, but is split into factions. Another example of the significance of seating arrangement is seen when an empty chair is always left next to certain members; those group members are probably being isolated by the rest of the group. Or if all couples in a group composed of couples sit together (the norm) with the exception of one, and these two sit one on each side of the leader, what theories might the observer want to test out through observing the session? Seating arrangement may or may not be significant, but the leader, as an observant group member, will want to use all possible group data available to help in improving group function.

Dates of the meetings should be recorded, since there may be need later to trace the sequence of progress from session to session. Also, the names of the group recorder and leader can be used to trace their development of group skills. The type of group and its purpose are recorded to aid readers who are not familiar with the group composition. Table 8-1 lists other data to be collected.

A *sociogram* can be developed from the seating arrangement chart; the number of comments made by each group member to each other group member or the group as a whole is tallied. The data can be reviewed to see who dominated the conversation, who spoke to whom, who is involved in pairing, who is an isolate, etc. When a sociogram is used, the person recording may be kept very busy drawing arrows from person to person indicating the direction of a comment and tallying responses.

TABLE 8-1 The Group Recording Guide

Events	Analysis of events	Leader action	Evaluation of leader actions	Alternative actions
All behaviors of group members:	Hunches about what the events seemed to mean:	What the leader did, including all behaviors listed in the Events column:	All hunches about why leader action was effective or ineffective:	All *specific* statements of how the leader might more effectively:
Words spoken Who speaks to whom Silences Gestures Tone of voice Increase or decrease in speech flow Eye contact Facial expressions Posture Body movements	Changes in group atmosphere Changes in cohesiveness Distortions of what occurred Feelings revealed Coping devices used Type and/or effect of silences Dependency Pairing Scapegoating Monopolizing		Introduction sufficient (insufficient) Group returned to focus of discussion (did not return) Tension decreased (increased) Leader's feelings interfered with action Communication skills used (not used)	

(continued)

TABLE 8-1 *(continued)*

Events	Analysis of events	Leader action	Evaluation of leader actions	Alternative actions
	Characteristic phase behavior Decisions reached Norms revealed Group disruption Competition		Less talkative people are (are not) talking Overtalkative people are quieter (more talkative) Apathy has decreased (increased) Goals defined (need definition) Leader placed responsibility with group (did not) Effective (ineffective) decision making Conflict decreased (increased) Nonuseful (useful) silence	Give responsibility to a group Increase security Keep action moving Restate Give information Clarify Point out Test for consensus Summarize Explore Get information Keep to topic

Cohesion increased
(decreased)
Scapegoating ends
(continues)
Competition ends
(continues)
Even (uneven) balance between task and maintenance functions
Themes
Transferences
Countertransferences

Events

Group events are all the behaviors of group members during a session except those of the formal or designated leader. Since informal leadership always occurs in groups to some degree, leadership behavior of informal leaders is placed in the Events column.

Words that are spoken should be placed in quotation marks, following the group member's number or initials:

EVENTS

H. G.   "That's a rotten thing to say. You really don't know what you're talking about."

Q. O.   "So what?"
Silence, 2 minutes.

T. Z.   "Well, what else is new?"

The group recorder strives to get word-for-word quotes from each speaker, unless the speaker repeats herself; then the group recorder may enter something like,

H. G.   "That's a rotten . . ." (repeats last speech).

It is suggested that novice recorders err on the side of recording everything they can, until an instructor or group process supervisor can review the recording and suggest observations that could be omitted. In general, all verbal and nonverbal interactions are relevant for understanding the ebb and flow of group interaction.

Analysis of Events

The Analysis of Events column should include all hunches about what an event seemed to mean. Not all events will have a clear meaning. However, when events are coupled, appear repeatedly, or appear to affect group interaction, guesses about their meaning can be made. For example, when each of a series of speeches by a group member is followed by a sudden, tense silence, the leader could hypothesize that the group atmosphere is changing (from cohesive to tense, or from informal to formal) in relation to that group member's behavior. Such hunches are useful because they give the nurse leader ideas about when and how to intervene in group interaction and when to remain silent.

However, since they are only hunches about the meaning of events, question marks can be placed before the analyses that require more supporting data. Examples of comments that might be placed in the Analysis of Events column are the following:

ANALYSIS OF EVENTS

    anxiety increasing
    rationalization
    helplessness
    intellectualization
    dependency on leader
? pairing
? scapegoating
    expected orientation behavior
? group moving into working phase decision reached by
        consensus unilateral decision
? group norm of politeness
? competition for leadership
? competition for leader approval
? theme: "We're deprived"
? theme: "We're different"
    informal leader behavior—summarizing
    informal leader behavior—giving feedback
    informal leader behavior—clarifying
    unclear—uses indefinite pronouns

Leader Action

The Leader Action column should include all verbal and nonverbal communications of the designated leader of the group. This column, then, together with column 1 (Events) should contain all the verbal and nonverbal interaction of the session. When written records are being kept, columns 1 and 3 are filled in during the group session. Columns 2, 4, and 5 are filled in after the group session is over.

Evaluation of Leader Action

Suggestions for comments that might be placed in this column indicate effective or ineffective action.

EVALUATION OF LEADER ACTION

effective—tension decreased
ineffective—? countertransference toward H. G.
effective—Q. R. started verbalizing feelings
ineffective—asked two questions at once
ineffective—asked a "yes/no" question
effective—redefined goals
effective—placed responsibility with the group
ineffective—insufficient introduction
ineffective—apathy continues
effective—decision reached by consensus
ineffective—conflict
ineffective—anxious silence followed
effective—cohesiveness increased
ineffective—uneven balance between task and maintenance functions
ineffective—nurse uses unclear pronouns

Alternative Actions

Suggestions for more effective leader behavior are placed in the Alternative Actions column. The purpose of this column is to provide a means of suggesting more concise, clear, and effective ways of intervening.

Some alternative action comments may be more concise restatements of what was said during the session. Others may be to remain silent or to provide needed actions, such as giving responsibility to the group, validating, pointing out time limits, providing support, giving feedback, keeping the group on its task, giving information, testing for consensus, summarizing, exploring, starting the group, and keeping on the topic. Examples of each of these suggestions, in the order listed here, are given below:

ALTERNATIVE ACTIONS

Remain silent
"Several group members seemed concerned about . . ." (to the group) "What's going on between Betty and Bob?"
"If I understand you right, you have mixed feelings about surgery."
"We have 10 minutes left to talk today."
"I guess I would feel upset, too."
"That sounds reasonable."
"Let's move on to discuss day care now."
"I'm Jan Shawn, a nurse. I'll be leading this group today."
"Are we all agreed then?"
"Today we covered how gastritis occurs and what different people do to decrease it."
"Say more about that"
"Let's all introduce ourselves"
"We're off the track; we were discussing birth control."

Table 8-2 shows a sample recording for a group of children who have diabetes. Notice the location of comments in each column of the recording. The interactions can be numbered to enable the reader to follow the comments in the sequence in which they were made.

USING RECORDINGS

Recording group interaction is a tedious but rewarding task. Students often complain about the time and effort

TABLE 8-2 Sample Recording of Group Interaction for Children with Diabetes

Events	Leader Analysis	Leader Action	Evaluation	Alternative Action
M shakes head No. P has parka over head, body turned away from M.	?Anxiety; expected behavior when a new member enters the group.	"Would you like to introduce yourself, M?"	Not a good question because it can be answered with yes or no.	"This is M, a new group member."
E, "I forgot." K, "There's a new injector for insulin. You pull the trigger."		"Perhaps E and K could help me tell the new member what we have discussed so far."	Shares responsibility with the group.	Leader could review; could ask members how they "feel about having a new member."
3-minute silence with group members moving in chairs.	Anxious silence.	"Uh huh, in a few minutes we'll get K to show us the gun."	Half-heartedly acknowledges K's remembrance of the last session.	"Yes, that's right; show us the injector."
H, "What time is this over?"	Anxious; wish to get away from uncomfortable	"I know we talked about food last week. What kind of diet is everyone on?"	Perhaps leader is anxious about how to deal with new member and so breaks the silence.	
		"The group is over in half an hour."	Task function of giving information.	

involved, but they also always comment on the helpfulness of recordings in learning group skills.

Recordings can be used in a number of ways. They can provide the learner with information about what happened in the group, what to observe in the future, and what would have been more effective leader action. Novice group leaders are often so busy participating in the group that they do not absorb these events and interactions unless recordings are made.

Recordings are often shared with a supervisor or instructor who can use the information about a leader's group skills to provide feedback. When this is to be done, space is left for supervisory comments to be inserted between events recorded.

Another use of recordings is to provide information to use in assessing the leader's progress in developing group skills. Table 8-3 shows a group skills checklist that can be used to evaluate leadership skills.

TABLE 8-3 Group Skills Checklist

Orientation Phase
 1. ____ Completes introductions
 2. ____ States purpose of group
 3. ____ Starts group action/keeps it moving
 4. ____ Brings information to the group
 5. ____ Gives feedback
 6. ____ Clarifies
 7. ____ Summarizes events
 8. ____ Helps group focus on task
 9. ____ Encourages clear, direct communication between members
10. ____ Diagnoses apathy and intervenes
11. ____ Diagnoses monopolizing and intervenes
12. ____ Diagnoses conflict and intervenes
13. ____ Diagnoses scapegoating and intervenes
14. ____ Places responsibility for decisions with group
15. ____ Identifies group norms
16. ____ Encourages ventilation of feelings
17. ____ Relieves tension
18. ____ Voices group feeling
19. ____ Identifies themes

(continued)

TABLE 8-3 (*continued*)

Working Phase
1. ____ Encourages description of problems or goals
2. ____ Encourages statement of alternate actions
3. ____ Allows group to do most of talking
4. ____ Helps group evaluate their decisions
5. ____ Tests for group consensus
6. ____ Identifies transferences and countertransferences

Termination Phase
1. ____ States length of group experience
2. ____ Reminds members that group experience will end in 2 sessions
3. ____ Assists group to discuss thoughts and feelings about the group ending
4. ____ Uses last group to summarize and evaluate group experience

Some instructors or supervisors may prefer that the learner abstract recording difficulties and group problems that need to be solved. Table 8-4 shows a report sheet that group members can use to abstract information from the complete group recording.

TABLE 8-4   Group Problems Report Sheet

Recording difficulties:

Group problems:
Describe specific examples of problems you found in the group you observed.

Consider these problems in terms of the following behaviors:
anxiety
conflict
apathy
decision making
task leadership
maintenance leadership
monopolizing
scapegoating

(*continued*)

TABLE 8-4 *(continued)*

---

pairing
cohesiveness
silences
dependency
disruptions
competition
themes
transferences/countertransferences

Still another way for the nurse group leader to gain group skills is to present group interaction recordings orally to an instructor and/or to a group of other nurses who are learning about group process. Entire recordings may be presented if time permits. If only 30 to 45 minutes are allowed for a presentation, the student can use the brief presentation form for group interaction, as shown in Table 8-5.

TABLE 8-5 Brief Presentation Form for Group Interaction

Divide your presentation of the following topics into four time segments:

1. Problems encountered with this group.

2. Themes (give one or two examples of each theme).

3. Transferences and countertransferences.

4. Problems (for which you need help).

SAMPLE RECORDINGS AND EVALUATIONS

Condensed examples of a session of a task group, a teaching group, and a supportive group follow. Each recording is evaluated in terms of leadership skills, and suggested interventions are offered.

A Task Group Recording

Table 8-6 presents the recording of a task group session.

Assessment of Group Leader's Effectiveness

The atmosphere of the group from beginning to end is one of casual communication; it is almost gossipy. This is not unexpected, since the participants have been classmates for two years. Perhaps because of relationships with her peers, the leader has difficulty establishing her leadership position in the group. Her very first comment indicates that she will give the group responsibility for making decisions. Unfortunately, there is no decision that is open to choice by the group, since the purpose of the group has already been established.

The casual atmosphere continues as members arrive late and share lunches. The leader makes no acknowledgment of the latecoming member. Some pairing occurs as members 7 and 9 develop a subgroup interaction. Next, the leader takes charge in an ineffective fashion. By making a unilateral decision about when decisions are to be reached and by suggesting how to proceed, the group is not encouraged to decide on how to plan its course. Perhaps as a reaction to this, member 3 states opposition to the leader's idea. At this point, member 5 shows anxiety and unsureness by questioning the recording procedure. The leader attempts to explore this query somewhat but does not clarify the group contract or elicit the member's concerns about recording. Next, tension is partially relieved by laughter and somewhat defused by returning to a topic that does not

TABLE 8-6 Recording of a Task Group Session

Seating Arrangement

Date: *3/18/81*

Group: *2ND Meeting*
Planning Committee for Class Follies

```
    7  8  9  1
 6              4 = leader
    5  4  3  2   1 = recorder
```

Events	Leader Analysis	Leader Action	Evaluation	Alternative Action
		"Do you want to talk about the Follies?"		Should not have given a choice.
7 "A skit could be made out of bedmaking."	7 Is involved and comfortable.			
9 arrives late; shares lunch with 8.	? Pairing.	"Today we're going to make definite decisions about what to include."	Task function of stating purpose.	
		"I thought we could use popular songs and have themes."		
3 "Oh, no."				
5 "Is 1 recording this?"		"Yes, is that O.K.?"		Leader could have reassured group that discussion was confidential.
Group laughs.				

(continued)

TABLE 8-6 (continued)

Events	Leader Analysis	Leader Action	Evaluation	Alternative Action
5 "We could impersonate faculty."	Group takes pressure off leader by returning to previous subject.	"Good idea. Some of you can do that."	Acknowledges suggestion and expands on it; part of decision-making process.	
4 "7 does; she imitates R real well!"	4 Becomes more active and makes first verbal comment.			
9 "I acted out a real vignette at work the other night."	9 and 8 pair off.			
8 "What happened?"				
7 "I'd like to do something like Truth is Stranger than Fiction."	Leadership function refocuses group to its task.			
9 "Oh, yes."				

8 "We could do our VW skit!"		?Cohesiveness increases.
6 "What about . . .?"	"Those all sound good. Let's have them one at a time."	Maintenance function of accepting task function of suggesting.
		Might have asked 2 to stay.
2 "I have to leave; see ya."	"Go ahead and tell us."	Refocus.
8 "I thought of another one; well, that's irrelevant."	"Don't you wonder if that will happen to you?"	Leader responds to 8's enthusiasm.
8 relates work incident.		Joins unrelated topic.
9 "It did." Group continues to discuss work incidents.	"We'll have to end soon."	Task function of giving information.

197

require members to take a stand against the leader and risk rejection.

The leader seems to benefit from the decrease in tension and is able to acknowledge a group member's suggestion, thereby rewarding making suggestions and promoting decision making and shared leadership. Group cohesiveness increases as member 4 joins in the task. At this point, the pairing activity of members 9 and 8 begins to interfere more seriously with group movement toward the goal. Member 7 asserts a leadership function and refocuses the group to its task. This action appears to increase cohesiveness again. The leader encourages movement toward the goal by rewarding and accepting suggestions, but fails to notice that member 2 has not participated actively in the group. Perhaps due to noninvolvement, that person leaves the group. The leader then switches from pursuit of the group goal to an unrelated topic. The group takes its cue from the leader, and from this point on the group makes no movement toward its goal.

Leadership skills during this task group session can be assessed to some extent. The leader seems able to tolerate anxiety within the group, but the levels were never very high. The leader is hesitant about establishing leadership, which may be due to unsureness and to unrealistic expectations about what the role entails; in such a situation a novice leader can become quite anxious, and consequently leadership skills will diminish. The leader does not exhibit any overt hostility or confronting behavior. The only incident that might lead to a confrontation occurs when number 3 says "Oh, no" in response to the leader's suggestion. Since neither person pursues the disagreement, no hostility develops.

Since it is not possible to know inner thoughts, the only way to evaluate how well the leader organizes and understands group process is to observe responses to the process. One clue here is the leader's response to member 5, who questions the recording procedure. By responding to this comment, the leader shows recognition of anxiety in the group. In the analysis, the leader also notes when member 4 begins to participate verbally in the group. When member 9 begins to discuss irrelevant work incidents, it is not clear whether the leader remains silent attempting to force the group to take responsibility for refocusing, or is unaware of the process that is occurring. Since this is only the second session of the group, it is unlikely that the leader has already taught group members to assume responsibility for leadership functions. It is possible, however, that member 7 has developed refocusing skills through other group experiences. When the leader joins in topics unrelated to the group purpose, it becomes clear there is a lack of understanding of the group process that is occurring.

The leader does seem to have spent some time thinking about the group goal and is probably aware of its importance to group process. This is evident from the third comment, when there is a suggested direction the group might take in working toward the goal.

The leader does not ask the group to assist with group functions, or record that the supervisor's assistance is requested. However, merely by using the process recording method, areas in which assistance is needed are clarified; and by giving the record to a supervisor or instructor, feedback can be obtained.

There are no examples of the leader's use of humor in the recording. Although the group members laugh at one point, this seems to be anxious laughter used to release tension.

The leader shows several signs of prompting independence in group members: allowing them to take leadership in refocusing the discussion, and promoting independence by telling them that they can share in developing skits to impersonate faculty members and that they can help to develop skit ideas one by one.

The leader seems to have mixed feelings about being a leader with peers. The task-leader functions of getting the group going, stating the group purpose, acknowledging and promoting exploration of suggestions, and giving information are only partially fulfilled. Some task functions that are not fulfilled (or not encouraged to be fulfilled) include clarifying the group task, keeping the group moving toward its goal, clarifying unclear statements, pointing out movement toward or away from the goal, restating, and teaching the group to solve problems.

The leader partially fulfills the maintenance function of acceptance by telling group members that they make good suggestions. One of the maintenance functions the leader does not fulfill (or encourage others to fulfill) is to give support to anxious or unsure members. For example, member 5 seems anxious about the recording procedure, and member 2 may have left due to anxiety. Other functions left unfilled are relieving tension, promoting attraction for the group, voicing group feeling, and helping the group to evaluate itself. This is not completely unexpected, since task group leaders often focus more intensively on the group goal and tend to ignore maintenance functions.

In the condensed group recording, the leader does not use the communication techniques of paraphrasing, behavior description, feeling description, or validating. Perhaps because the leader is so involved in the group task and work incidents, she focuses more on stating the purpose, decision making, and giving information.

The leader records no reactions to group processes. This is probably understandable in the beginning leader, who is preoccupied with directing the group and ensuring that the mechanical aspects of group structure are fulfilled. However, as leaders progress in their development of leadership skills, it is expected that they will begin to be more aware of their thoughts and feelings about what happens in the group, and of how they respond to group members' attempts to cast them in a role or to evoke under- or overreactions.

How could the leader intervene to make this task group session more constructive and fruitful? An assessment of leadership skills can serve as a guide to the supervisor or instructor in suggesting possible interventions to the nurse group leader. Some of the functions the leader of this group did not fulfill have already been discussed.

One suggested intervention in this instance might be for the leader to provide a clearer statement of the group goal or purpose. For example, the leader needs to be more specific about decisions the group is to make during that session; for example, "We're here to agree on five skits to include in the Class Follies." Another way to clarify the group goal would be to ascertain group members' reactions to the stated goal by asking outright, "What are your feelings about completing that task today?"

In these examples and in the interventions that follow, the leadership function could be provided by the designated leader or by one of the other group members. The leader might ask a group member to state (or restate) the group purpose, and to ask for feedback, or a group member might volunteer to state the group purpose and to test for group reactions. In some groups, the designated leader may not be the most skilled of the members in assuming group functions and/or may not have taught others how to assume group functions.

Although the leader notes that member 5 is concerned about the recording, no specific alternative action is suggested. One that could be used is, "This information on the recording is shared only with my supervisor for learning purposes. How do you feel about having this meeting recorded?"

The next significant event not dealt with by the leader is the leave-taking of number 2. If this person's silence is observed early in the session, the leader might try to draw the silent member into the group by saying, "What are you thinking about?" or "What is your reaction to this discussion?" Even if the leader does miss the silent member's clues, a comment when the member is about to leave can be made, such as, "Leaving?" or "We only have 15 minutes left today, and we really need your input." Sometimes just by questioning the leave-taking, or by reinforcing the members' commitment to the group, the leader can promote attraction for the group and the common good.

Another event that requires the leader's intervention is

the switch in group focus from the group goal to work incidents. In this case, the leader might comment, "We're off the track," or "Tell us after the meeting," or "let's get back to the skits for the Follies."

Some of the missing leader functions may be the result of inexperience in acting as group leader. Others may be due to the leader's inability to cope with mixed feelings about being leader in a group of peers. A suggested preventive intervention would be for the leader to examine his or her reactions to members. Although it is often useful to be liked by group members, this is not always a prerequisite to the leader's helpfulness to a group. If the need to be accepted, liked, and approved by group members exceeds or equals the wish to be helpful, the leader's need may interfere with effective leading of the group. For these reasons, leaders would be well advised to seek out supervision from a more experienced group leader until they have gained considerable experience.

Assessment of Group Recorder's Skills

The group recorder has reported seating arrangement, date of the meeting, the names of the leader and the recorder, and the purpose of the group. Events and leader actions are clearly stated. Quotation marks are used to separate verbal statements from nonverbal communications. The Analysis of Events column contains no observed behaviors; analyses that have little data to support them are preceded by question marks.

This recording could be improved by making two changes. First, observations regarding lack of leader reactions to the group could be placed in the fourth column. Examples of comments that could have been included in that column are, "Vying with group member for leadership," "Angry with group member," and "Anxious about beginning the group."

Second, specific statements or behaviors are called for in the fifth column. Instead, the suggestions found there are general in nature. Specific alternative actions that might be suggested are, "Let's talk about the Follies," "The recordings will be shared only with my supervisor," "Leaving?" and "Tell us after the meeting is over."

A Teaching Group Recording

Table 8-7 presents the recording of an early session of a teaching group. The focus of the group is on teaching pregnant women about physiological, anatomical, and emotional changes that occur during pregnancy, and on physical exercises that are useful during pregnancy, labor, and delivery.

Assessment of Group Leader's Effectiveness

From the beginning of the session, there is no casualness or socializing in this group. The leader gets right down to business and even omits important orienting information. The atmosphere of the session is formal as the nurse teacher starts by imparting information and the group members by asking for information. Not unexpectedly, themes of anxiety and conflict are noticeable in this early group session.

Member A is the most verbal group member. Although the talkativeness creates no problems at this point, it is a signal to the leader to watch for the process of monopolizing. Member A's behavior may also be viewed as that of group spokesman; anxiety is not an unusual reaction to anticipated delivery, and member A may be voicing a fear that others in the group share.

The group continues, and the previous leader arrives unexpectedly while they are practicing breathing exercises. At this point a disruption occurs, as the leader's focus of attention shifts from the group to working out a coleading relationship. Because neither the leader nor the ex-leader deals with this issue directly, most of the rest of the session is used to work it out indirectly.

TABLE 8-7 Recording of a Teaching Group Session for Expectant Mothers

Seating Arrangement   Date: 3/21/97

D   J   A   N = leader   Group: Prenatal Teaching Group
     N   M   M = recorder

Events	Leader Analysis	Leader Action	Evaluation	Alternative Action
			No introduction of new group leader.	"I'm the new leader for today."
A giggles.	Anxiety.	"Do you know what to expect when labor begins?"	A yes/no question.	"Who can tell us the signs of labor beginning?"
		"There are several signs; one is the bloody show, another is the breaking of waters."		
A "I was wondering because I dribble when I sneeze; is that urine or	A voices a potential source of anxiety.	"It was probably not the waters; have you felt crampy?"	Clarifies; seeks information.	"Anyone in the group have an answer?" or "Urine is yellow; if you wear a Kotex you can

A "I read about those."	?Seeking leader approval.	"Those are probably the Braxton Hicks contractions we talked about."	Clarifying; seeking information; giving information.	"Perhaps you could tell the group what you read."
		Refers to course outline.	Some anxiety; retreats to paper.	
A "Yesterday I felt the baby pushing. It scared me."	Theme: anxiety about delivery.	"If you feel nervous, sit down and relax."	Gives solution for A's fear. Could have explored this further.	"What scared you?" or "Being scared is a natural reaction" or "Have others felt scared?"
		"Do you want to practice Kegel exercises?"	A yes/no question.	"Let's practice Kegel exercises; they prevent dripping urine."
Members lie on floor and practice muscle control and breathing exercises.		Leader coaches and gives each feedback on how each has mastered the exercise.	A delayed response, but effective in reinforcing and evaluating learner's exercise abilities.	

(continued)

TABLE 8-7 (continued)

Events	Leader Analysis	Leader Action	Evaluation	Alternative Action
J enters and exercising stops.	Disruption by member who comes late.		Leader does not acknowledge entrance.	"J's here. She usually leads the group. Do you want to take over now, J?"
			?Conflict and/or competition.	
Group resumes exercises, J starts coaching them.		"That's right, D."	Vying for leadership but does not settle how to work together directly.	
Members turn first to J and then to N for help. J "The students can help you."	Group unclear about who is leader. J differentiates leader from students.	"Do you want this seat, J?"	N defers leadership to J without discussing it; could use this situation to teach shared leadership.	"I'll help with the exercises. Do you want to do the talking, J?"

Leadership skills during the teaching group session can be assessed to some extent. The leader seems to have an adequate tolerance for anxiety and is able to observe, identify, and focus on expressed anxiety. Labeling the member's feeling as "nervousness" gives the leader an opening to suggest possible interventions, such as sitting down and practicing relaxation exercises when anxious.

There are no evidences of hostility among group members. If anything, extreme dependency and compliance are demonstrated as the members turn continually to the leader for advice and assistance. The leader, in turn, demonstrates her dependency on J by deferring to her as if she were the authority, rather than giving her feedback about how to work together. J accepts the authoritarian role, thus passing up a chance to show the group how to establish a collaborative relationship by discussing this situation in the group.

By identifying and intervening in anxiety, the leader demonstrates an understanding of that group process. She also seems to recognize symptoms of dependency when she speculates that member A may be seeking leader approval. Whether the leader understands the process of what occurs between herself and the previous leader at the time that this is happening is less clear. There are additional written notes speculating on how this disruption is affecting both the group and the designated leader. It may be that the leader (or recorder) only understands the conflict/competition process after reviewing the written record of the session. Nevertheless, both observations are astute and lead to useful alternative actions after the fact, if not to actual interventions at the time the event occurred.

There is only indirect evidence that the leader made any preparations for leading the group. She seemed prepared in terms of teaching content and of trying to use and apply group process theory to group events, but apparently she had not thought much about or was unable to implement a smooth beginning for the session.

In her first comment, the leader asks the group to assist

with group functions by asking them for information. Most of the rest of her comments seem to be attempts to provide leadership functions herself, except when she defers to J, the ex-leader.

Neither the leader nor the group recorder requests assistance. However, merely recording and turning in a written record is one way of asking for assistance from a more experienced group leader. There are no examples of humor in this recording. On the contrary, an atmosphere of seriousness prevails.

The leader makes no attempt to promote independence in group members. One wonders whether she is aware that she may be promoting member A's dependent bids for attention by not encouraging group members to take more responsibility for group functioning.

The leader seems to move easily into the traditional teaching role. Most of her statements are of an information-giving or -gathering nature. The leader fulfills the task functions of getting the group going and clarifying unclear statements. Some task functions she does not fulfill are stating the group purpose, acknowledging and exploring group members' suggestions, keeping the group moving toward its goal, pointing out movement toward or away from the group goal, restating, and teaching the group to solve problems.

The leader fulfills the maintenance functions of accepting (by telling D she was doing an exercise correctly) and of giving support (by suggesting a solution for member A's anxiety). She may be trying to relieve high tension levels in the group by suggesting a release through physical exercise. Some maintenance functions the leader does not fill are voicing group feeling, promoting attraction for the group, and helping the group to evaluate itself. Unlike the leader in the foregoing task group recording, this leader does make an attempt to balance task functions with maintenance functions.

The leader does not use paraphrasing, behavior description, feeling description, or validating. She does use feedback by telling member D that she is doing an exercise correctly.

A specific communication problem is demonstrated by the use of yes/no questions. Since the leader's role involves facilitating communication, it is important for her to speak as little as possible and to allow others to speak more frequently. When the leader uses yes/no questions, the group members answer with a brief yes or no.

In the beginning of the session, the leader has a tendency to give information rather than to find out what group members already know and what they could teach one another. Then, when the previous leader enters, the present leader directs observation and communication primarily toward her, but in an indirect manner. Thus, neither serves as a role model by teaching the group how to work out a collaborative relationship, nor do they concentrate on being effective communicators with group members.

The leader recorded several of her own reactions to group events. First, she notes her anxiety when perceiving a challenge to give information about Braxton Hicks contractions. Perhaps because she feels unsure about her knowledge in this area, she retreats to her course outline to decrease her anxiety. Second, the leader recognizes the delay between A's expressed concern about losing urine and the leader's suggestion that the group practice Kegel exercises. Third, after the group session, the leader identifies her feelings of conflict about competition with the other leader.

What interventions could be made to improve group functioning? First of all, the leader of this formal, serious group could well consider introducing some fun, lightness, and relaxation into the situation. By using warming-up exercises along with humor, the leader could give the group atmosphere a much happier tone. Also, if the leader feels comfortable doing so, she could share her own thoughts and feelings as a way of increasing cohesiveness and decreasing formality.

Independence in group members could be promoted by

asking them to share information with one another, to turn to one another—rather than the leader—for assistance, and to participate in problem-solving efforts. This will require the leader to step out of the role of "expert" and share leadership functions with the group, a difficult thing for the novice group leader to do when she is struggling to learn the basic mechanics of directing a group. It might be helpful for her to comment, "Who has an answer for that?" or "Tell us what you read." Both statements will increase independent action by prompting group members to provide information.

Some maintenance functions could be filled by the leader making such comments as, "I wonder if others in the group are worried about dribbling urine?" or "I wonder what feelings others have about delivery?" or "I'm not sure what to do here, J; I'm not sure how we should work out our relationship as leaders."

In the task function area the leader could state the group purpose more clearly at the beginning of the session. She might say, "This is the third meeting of the prenatal teaching group. Tonight we will focus on your concerns about delivery," or "This is our third meeting. Our focus tonight is anticipated labor problems, and how you plan to deal with them." Because the leader is unclear about the focus of her teaching, the content shifts from labor to problems of pregnancy to delivery to exercise practice. Although a leader must be flexible enough to respond to emerging group needs, it is always helpful to plan what will be covered during that teaching session. If the leader has a plan and refocuses on the issues at hand, the anxious member's potentially monopolizing behavior can be reduced. She can also direct the discussion to the topic of the meeting by asking others for their reactions about that topic. With the session proceeding as it is, only member A is able to verbalize her feelings. By trying to link others' responses to member A's statements, a discussion rather than a dialogue may ensue. Sample statements that may be beneficial in reversing the dialogue situation are, "Who else has an idea about that?" or "What's your reaction to what A said?"

The leader shows unsureness about how to proceed by asking the group to decide how to begin and structure the group. Also, the way she words her questions demonstrates some weakness in communication skills. It is possible to structure group events and get feedback from the group at the same time. For example, the leader could say, "Let's begin talking about labor. What thoughts do you have about what to expect?" or, "We could practice the exercise right now that decreases urine dribbling; what's your reaction to this idea?" Neither of these questions can be answered with a simple yes or no, and thus they encourage the group to share ideas and participate in decision making.

Assessment of Group Recorder's Skills

The initial information about seating arrangement, date, and so on seems to be appropriate. Events and leader actions are clearly recorded. Verbal communication has been placed in quotation marks to differentiate it from nonverbal communication. The analysis of events contains proper information since only the leader's ideas about what occurred are recorded there.

The record shows that the leader and/or group recorder have spent time thinking about and evaluating their feelings about group events. The ability to observe oneself objectively is a group skill of high order. Specific statements are recorded in the Alternative Action column. In general, this recording demonstrates a high level of skill.

A Supportive Group Recording

Table 8-8 represents the recording of a supportive group or "rap session" for adolescents who have diabetes. The focus of the group is on sharing interpersonal situations and knowledge related to the diabetic experience.

TABLE 8-8 Recording of a Supportive Group for Adolescents with Diabetes

Seating Arrangement

Date: 3/25/84

Group: *Rap Session for Adolescents with Diabetes*

```
  3   4
2       5
1
  8   7   6
```

7 = leader
8 = recorder

Events	Leader Analysis	Leader Action	Evaluation	Alternative Action
All members look at leader.		Reviews group contract. Leans forward on chair with hands partially covering face.	Task function of getting group going. Mixed message via body language.	Remove hands from face.
	Dependency and low-level self-disclosure characteristic of orientation phase.	"Let's go around the group introducing ourselves."	Leader could encourage more disclosure.	"What else would you like us to know about you?"
Members state their names but look at leader while doing so; all deny difficulties with diabetes.		"I think it's interesting that no one's been hampered by diabetes."	Tries to increase cohesiveness by pointing out similarity.	"No problems at all because you have diabetes?"
6 "I had a teacher once who acted like I had a contagious disease."	6 Decreases group tension.	"How did you feel then?"	Could introduce doubt to decrease denial. Leader tries to explore feeling.	"Have others had a similar reaction?"

Group interaction	Observations / dynamics	Leader response	Analysis	Intervention
3 "I try to keep it a secret from teachers."	?Group compares leader with other authority figures.	"Sounds like some teachers could use some health teaching themselves."	Supports 3, but may be over-protective due to irritation with teachers.	"How come?"
4 "Most of my friends know. There's one teacher who refers to it as my problem."	Potential monopolizing member; may be seeking approval or recognition.		Need to try to relate 3's difficulties to others'.	"Anyone else feel as 3 does?" or "What does the group think about what 3 is saying?"
3 Proceeds with long monologue with theme of being misunderstood especially about diet.				
2 "I always have food hidden in my room."	Level of self-disclosure deepens with sharing of a secret.	"You have something in common." Goes on to discuss why diet is important.		
6 and 4 "Me too!"	Cohesiveness increasing in most of group members.		Promotes cohesiveness then tries to retain leadership by redirecting the focus; is leader anxious here?	Silence.
General discussion about sneaking food.				

(continued)

TABLE 8-8 (*continued*)

Events	Leader Analysis	Leader Action	Evaluation	Alternative Action
3 Looks at leader and does not join in.				
6 "No matter what's wrong, my mother says it's due to diabetes." Looks at leader.	May be testing to see if leader will respond as mother does.	"Do you resent that?"	Labels feeling without validating it.	"What's your reaction to that?"
5 "I always know when I'm going to have a reaction."	First time 5 spoke. 3 and 1 are potential isolates in this group.	"Let's talk a little about reactions."	Seeks to explore a topic.	
All but 3 and 1 join in a discussion of reactions.		"Time's up for today. See you next week."	Takes responsibility for ending group.	"Let's summarize what happened today."

Assessment of Group Leader's Effectiveness

Of the three sample recordings that have been presented, this one reveals the highest level of self-disclosure. Perhaps this finding is not completely unexpected, since supportive groups zero in on personal thoughts and feelings. However, the leader also demonstrates a level of communication skill and ease that the other two leaders did not.

The leader discharges her responsibility by reviewing the group contract and encouraging all group members to participate by sharing in introductions. Member dependency and low self-disclosure occurs when they initially look to the leader and deny difficulties with diabetes. When the leader assists group process by pointing to how similar they are in their reactions to diabetes, the potential for group cohesiveness increases, and there is greater freedom to discuss difficulties. Tension is further released through group laughter, which may be laughter of recognition; group members may have shared the experiences of being treated differently because of their diabetes.

It is not unusual for group members to perceive the group leader as a teacher. For this reason it is possible that the discussion about teachers may be an attempt to compare and contrast the leader's responses to other authority figures' behavior. Some thoughts group members may be having in this area are: Will this person be like other adults I know? Will I be understood here? Can I be safe and comfortable here so I can share my thoughts and feelings? Instead of recognizing this process, the leader sides with the students and makes a slightly derogatory comment about the teacher.

The leader shows some irritation, and a monologue concerning being misunderstood follows. It could be that the members feel that the leader misinterpreted their earlier testing behavior of comparing authority figures, and so member 3 speaks for the group and tells about feeling misunderstood. Also member 3's behavior may be seen as monopolizing. The leader seems not to recognize or at least not to know how to deal with monopolizing as it occurs. Perhaps the leader's silence was helpful because members 2, 4, and 6 feel secure enough to share a secret. With this increase in self-disclosure, group cohesiveness increases. At the same time, member 3 continues to try to have a special relationship with the leader, as exemplified by the fact that she does not join in the secret-sharing activity and looks toward the leader instead.

Perhaps the leader becomes anxious with the level of self-disclosure shown, because no sooner has she increased cohesiveness and sharing than she increases distance in the group by taking the teacher role of information-giver. Member 6 continues testing to see if the leader is like other authority figures—in this case, his mother. The leader tries to explore the member's relationship with his mother, but she puts some words into his mouth by labeling his feeling as resentment rather than by allowing him to describe his own feeling.

Despite the leader's action, member 5, who has been silent until now, is able to assert herself as an independent person who knows as well as her mother when she is going to have a hypo- or hyperglycemic reaction. It is interesting that member 5 chooses this point at which to speak. It may be that this person has been observing the others' behavior, including the leader's, and only now feels comfortable enough to join in. Or number 6's comment may be one that number 5 can identify with. The leader makes a judgment at this time that the topic of reactions has relevance for the whole group and so tries to explore it further. In the process of this group, as in all groups, a number of events occur during the session that make it necessary for the leader to decide when and how to intervene. Part of this decision-making process is based on theory and timing; part of it is related to the leader's personal style and experience in handling various group events.

As the session ends, the leader introduces more structure into the group by calling attention to the end of the meeting. She also encourages its ongoing quality by stating her intention to see the members at the next session.

There are three times during this meeting when the leader's anxiety has potential for influencing group process. The first occurs at the beginning of the session, when the leader gives a mixed communication message. The verbal message is "I am open and interested," while the nonverbal message is "I am closed off and distant." It is quite likely that this mixed message is caused by the leader's anxiety. If the leader's ability to tolerate anxiety were evaluated on the basis of this message alone, the conclusion would be that the leader might have shown more tolerance for anxiety had she not given a mixed message and had she been able consciously to remove her hands from her face.

The second occurrence of anxiety is less clear. It is probable that the leader experiences some anxiety when member 6 brings up the example of being mistreated by a teacher who "acted like I had a contagious disease." The leader's anxiety then may be due to her unmet but unrealistic expectations of teachers, to the member's attempt to evoke a sympathetic response from the leader, or to some other reaction. Despite the cause, it is fairly clear that leader anxiety is converted into irritation or anger; such conversion is not unusual and is the kind that group leaders need to watch for in themselves and in other group members. If the leader had a higher tolerance for anxious feelings, she might not have to convert her discomfort into irritation or anger.

The third time the leader's anxiety is evident is when she deflects the group focus from disclosure and cohesiveness to a more neutral topic. Changing topics is a common reaction to anxiety. Again, if the leader had a greater tolerance for anxiety, she might not need to change the subject and thereby increase distance between herself and the group. Anxiety is more likely to occur in a less structured group, such as a supportive one, where guidelines for behavior are less clear and the expectations of higher levels of self-disclosure can increase discomfort. For these reasons, the leader of a supportive group needs to be especially skilled in identifying and dealing with anxiety in self and others.

There are no examples of hostility among group members; all seem to be trying to get along with one another and to impress the leader. This is expected behavior in early group sessions.

The group recorder's analyses of events and evaluation of leader action give some clues to how well the leader understands group process. There is evidence of application of group theory and of such concepts as dependency, self-disclosure, monopolizing, cohesiveness, testing, isolation, communication, and denial. The leader also demonstrates an ability to understand her own anxiety and irritation in reaction to group processes.

There is only indirect evidence that the leader had thought through how to proceed with the group session. For example, she begins the group effectively by reviewing the group contract and starting group introductions. She also has decided how to end the group. The middle part of the session seems to have been less well thought out; at one point the leader begins to teach about diabetic diets; whether this is due to insufficient preplanning or spur-of-the-moment anxiety is not clear.

The leader asks the group to share in introductions. She makes some attempt to get group members to talk to one another when she points out their similarities, but she could make more attempts to have group members ask one another questions and react to comments, rather than expecting the leader to direct and comment on what is said.

Neither the leader nor the group recorder requests any assistance. However, producing a written record is itself one way the inexperienced leader can ask for assistance.

Although there is laughter in this group, it is unclear whether humor is intended. Here, as in the task group recording (Table 8-6), laughter may be primarily tension-relieving behavior. In this case, exaggeration is a factor in the member's comments, and this could be the basis for the laughter. The leader herself makes no use of humor during the session.

The leader promotes independence by asking group members to introduce themselves and by suggesting that the group explore diabetic reactions more thoroughly. Both of these actions imply that the leader considers the group members as capable of performing these tasks.

In the Alternative Action column the leader makes further suggestions about how she could have promoted independence. She says she could have asked the group to compare and contrast their reactions ("Have others had a similar reaction?" and "Anyone else feel as 3 does?"), or to summarize what happened or what they accomplished in that group session.

When the leader remains silent, the group is forced to take responsibility for group functioning. Thus, silence can be an effective method of encouraging the group to take responsibility for keeping the group process moving. Here, the leader is able to let go partially of the directing reins. When self-disclosure becomes uncomfortable for her, she again takes firm hold.

The leader takes some or all of the responsibility for the task functions of getting the group going, stating the group purpose, giving information, acknowledging and exploring group members' suggestions, keeping the group moving toward its goal, and ending the group. She demonstrates little direction in terms of restating, summarizing, and teaching the group to solve problems.

The leader fulfills the maintenance functions of accepting, supporting, and promoting attraction for the group by pointing out similarities between group members and by exploring feelings. She does not fill the maintenance functions of voicing group feeling and helping the group to evaluate itself, but she makes some attempt to achieve a balance between task and maintenance functions.

The leader does not use the communication techniques of paraphrasing, behavioral description, or validating. Instead of validating member 6's feeling, she labels the feeling herself. Her statement about noting that no one seems hampered by having diabetes could be viewed as a feedback statement.

One of the leader's questions is of the yes/no variety. When she asks, "Do you resent that?" her wording is ineffective for two reasons. First, the question is one that can be answered with a brief yes or no. Second, the question implies a way member 6 is expected to feel; if he does not already feel that way, the leader may be suggesting how she thinks he should feel. If the group member is quite susceptible to the influence of authority figures, he may answer yes just to receive the leader's approval.

The leader has a tendency to focus on individual problems within the group setting. The result is that she not only promotes dependency on herself (since communications are structured to go between her and another group member) but also carries on a series of one-to-one relationships under the guise of dealing with the group. She may recognize this trait after the fact, because many of her Alternative Action comments suggest ways to involve group members with one another: "Have others had a similar reaction?" "Anyone else feel as 3 does?" and, "What does the group think about what 3 is saying?"

The leader notes three of her reactions to the group. First, she points out that she gave the group a mixed message. She does not identify the feeling that led to the discordant verbal/nonverbal message, but it is likely that she recognizes it as anxiety. Such leader reaction would not be unexpected in the early part of the first group session. Had the leader noted this on her recording, it would have provided even further evidence that she is knowledgeable about group process.

Second, the leader is aware of feelings of protectiveness toward member 3. Awareness of countertransference reactions is helpful; there would be even stronger evidence of the leader's grasp of her reactions if the recording had included a statement concerning need for further supervision in this area and/or intent to pay attention to future interactions of this type with member 3.

Third, the leader recognizes that she may be anxious because the group has a high level of self-disclosure. Perhaps she feels left out or is worried that she will not be able to control how much personal material will be shared. To some extent, the leader does need to balance levels of self-disclosure so that cohesiveness is increased, yet embarrassment or high anxiety does not result. If only one group member were disclosing secrets, the leader could certainly want either to encourage others to share similar experiences or to defuse the intensity of the disclosure so that other group members will not become frightened. In this case, four of the six group members are openly sharing with one another; it therefore seems that the leader's shift to the more neutral topic of diet is primarily to meet her own inclusion or control needs.

This assessment of leader skills suggests alternative methods of handling similar group situations in the future. One suggested intervention is that the leader should study and ask for ongoing supervision regarding her tendency to overprotect and control the group. In the process of doing so, the leader may be able to encourage more independence among group members by asking them to describe, identify, explore, and suggest alternative ways of dealing with interpersonal reactions to having diabetes. Some statements that illustrate this kind of leader intervention are: "How has each of you reacted when others have . . .?", "What feeling is it that you all are talking about?", "Let's have all the group members tell a little more about their experiences with . . .," and "What other ways could you handle that situation in the future?"

The record suggests one comment that might have made the leader more effective in helping the group to summarize the session. Other comments she might have used are: "Today we got acquainted a little bit and began to talk about how people who don't have diabetes react to those who do. We also touched on diet and diabetic reactions. I think all three of these topics are important and that we could expand on them in future sessions." Since this is the first session of the group, it may be too early to expect group members to summarize. It is suggested that the leader act as role model for the group by summarizing the first few sessions. After that, the leader might say, "Who would like to summarize what we did today?" If no one volunteers, the leader can again summarize but add, "Summarizing is an important skill; you learn it through practice, and the group is a good place to begin." This kind of statement does not imply punishment to group members who do not volunteer, but it does point out the leader's expectations and provide a guideline for group behavior in future sessions.

Although many of the alternative action comments are stated well, some could be added or expanded. For example, the leader could suggest some alternative ways to ask the group to discuss their diabetic reactions. Two examples are: "Who wants to begin talking about his reactions?" and, "Let's go around the group and share experiences in this area."

Assessment of Group Recorder's Skills

The initial information about seating arrangement, date, and so on is adequate. Events and leader actions are clearly recorded. Verbal communication has been placed in quotation marks to differentiate it from nonverbal communication. The analysis of events contains appropriate information, since only the leader's ideas about what occurred are recorded.

The amount of information in columns 2, 4, and 5 provides evidence that the leader and/or group recorder have thought about group events and leader reactions. They make an effort to separate events—or what is observed in the group—from analysis and evaluation—or what the leader/recorder thinks and feels about what happens in the group. In general, this record shows excellent recording ability.

READINGS

Bradford, L. Stock, D., & Horowitz, M. (1976). How to diagnose group problems. In S. Stone, M. Berger, D. Elhart, S. Firsich, & S. Jordan (Eds.). *Management for nurses*. St. Louis: Mosby.

Brooks, D. (1976). Teletherapy: or how to use videotape feedback to enhance group process. *Perspectives in Psychiatric Care 14*, 83–87.

Cain, E. (1986). Psychosocial benefits of a cancer support group. *Cancer 57* (1), 183–189.

Chopra, A. (1973). Motivation in task-oriented groups. *Journal of Nursing Administration 3*, 55.

Clark, C. (1975) *Recording and evaluating nurse-patient interactions: Using the process recording guide*. Garden Grove, CA: Trainex Press.

Cooper, S. (1973). Committees that work. *Journal of Nursing Administration 3*, 30.

Dodge, C. (1969). A review of the use of audiovisual equipment in psychotherapy. *Perspectives in Psychiatric Care 7*, 248–258.

Gregorie, J. & Swanson, D. (1975). Group sessions for the wives of home hemodialysis patients. *American Journal of Nursing 75*, 633–635.

Heller, V. (1973). Handicapped patients talk together. In A. Roa & M. Sherwood (Eds.), *Nursing in the 70's*. New York: Wiley.

Johnson, D. & Johnson, F. (1975). Leading discussion groups. In D. Johnson & F. Johnson (Eds.), *Joining together: group theory and group skills*. Englewood Cliffs, NJ: Prentice-Hall.

Kliban, M. et al. (1984). Bereavement counseling in groups . . . hospice care includes followup for survivors. *Caring 3* (9), 12–18.

Lukse, M. (1985). The effect of group counseling on the frequency of grief reported by infertile couples. *Journal of Obstetrics, Gynecological and Neonatal Nursing 14* (6)(Suppl.), 675–705.

McCann, M. (1976). Group sessions for families of post-coronary patients. *Supervisor Nurse 7*, 17–19.

Moynihan, R. et al. (1984). Nursing support groups in a cancer center. *Journal of Psychosocial Oncology 2* (1), 33–48.

Muecke, M. (1970). Videotape Recordings: A tool for psychiatric clinical supervision. *Perspectives in Psychiatric Care 8*, 200–208.

Parsall, S. (1974). Cancer patients help each other. *American Journal of Nursing 74*, 650–651.

Radtke, M. & Wilson, A. (1973). Team conferences that work. *American Journal of Nursing 73*, 506–508.

Salzer, J. (1975). Classes to improve diabetic self-care. *American Journal of Nursing 75,* 1324–1326.

Smith, E. D. (1971). Group conferences for postpartum patients. *American Journal of Nursing 71,* 112–113.

Smyth, K. (1971). Symposium on Patient Teaching. *Nursing Clinics of North America 6,* 571–806.

Stephens, B. (1976). Use of groups for management. *First-Line Patient Care Management.* Wakefield, MA: Contemporary Publishing.

Stoller, F. (1972). The use of videotape feedback. In L. Solomon & B. Berzon (Eds.). *New Perspectives in Encounter Groups.* New York: Jossey-Bass.

Wilson, L. (1970). Listening. In (Coord.) C. Carlson. *Behavioral Concepts and Nursing Intervention.* Philadelphia: Lippincott.

Wittmeyer, A. (1971). Teaching by Audiotape. *Nursing Outlook 19,* 162–163.

Wolff, I. (1972), Acceptance. *American Journal of Nursing 72,* 1412–1415.

9
When the Organization is the Group

THE HIGHLY CREATIVE ORGANIZATION

A key question for nurse leaders in organizations is "How do I go about working with people in such a way that it releases their creative energies?" All organizations can benefit from actions that will develop more creative solutions to problems. Although many administrators may say they value creativity, forces often push the organization toward the status quo and short-term solutions. The creative individual may have difficulty adapting to a noncreative work environment. Dyer (1976, p. 116) has compared characteristics of the creative individual with those of the creative organization. Creative individuals tend to produce a large number of original ideas quickly, are motivated by their interest in a problem, are able to suspend their judgment long enough to make adequate analysis and exploration, are relativistic rather than authoritarian, are playful and undisciplined when working, are independent rather than conforming in judgment, view themselves as different, and have a rich fantasy life and superior reality orientation. Creative organizations have many of the same characteristics; they have open channels of communication, allow eccentricity, evaluate ideas based on their merit not on the status of the originator, use long-range planning, experiment with new ideas without prejudging them, are decentralized and diversified, encourage risk-taking and are tolerant of error, allow freedom to choose and pursue problems and discuss ideas, value original and different objectives, and provide a stable, secure environment that allows creators to roam.

Leaders are often rewarded for having a smooth-working, functioning system. How can the nurse leader encourage creativity, which may at times appear jagged and uneven or even crazy to the uninvolved observer? Unfortunately, many creative individuals are pressured to conform and their creative gifts may not be used. Many organizations of which the nurse is a part may have a reasonable level of trust and do a fine job; their problem may be primarily that they are using old, nonuseful solutions to new problems. Dyer (1976, pp. 121–122) suggests the following elements for developing a program that stimulates creativity: analyze the current level of innovation and employees' desire or need for more creative work; plan actions for stimulating innovation, including seminars on creative thinking; provide incentives for new, productive ideas; encourage brainstorming in staff meetings; create think tanks; include creativity in performance reviews; develop policies that reduce fear of making a mistake; keep staff openly informed about organizational problems that need solving; have a reward system for the creative person; have an outside observer assess creative output and suggest ways of innovating; rotate people to different parts of the organization so there are new mixtures of people working on old problems; have job enrichment sessions so staff can devise ways of enriching their own jobs.

DIAGNOSING ORGANIZATIONAL SYSTEMS

A first step in moving toward a creative, innovative organization is diagnosis. There are three parts of an *organizational system* that need to be assessed: the social system, the operation system and the administrative system.

The *social system* has basic components including: climate or prevailing emotional state (formal, relaxed, defensive, cautious, accepting, trusting), communication network (formal and informal patterns about who talks with whom, when, how often, and about what), status-role structure (division of labor, who holds power, has influence, and how this is achieved), pattern of management (style of handling superordinate and subordinate action), decision-making method (consensus, authoritarian, democratic), values and goals (what are the priorities in the system, how are these established, how well do members accept them and work toward them).

The *operation system* includes all the methods of getting the work done. Each organization has a unique way of arranging equipment, people, material, and processes to accomplish the work. Often, it is difficult to separate the social system processes from operation system processes—they interact. However, there are unique elements of the operation system such as how furniture is arranged, how work space is used, where supplies are stored, and so forth. Although all hospital units may be furnished with the same furniture, on one unit the staff may form a circle to meet and on another, most may stand or do their paper work while the head nurse sits and gives a report. The circular arrangement of furniture (operation system) can affect the level of interaction (social system), but even in a circular arrangement, it is possible for a head nurse who wants to lecture or carry on a monologue to do so.

The *administrative system* interlaces the social and operation systems and is a network of procedures, policies, reports, and audits. Important elements in the administrative system are hiring, firing and promotional methods, fringe benefits (vacations, sick leave, retirement, insurance, leave time), salaries, bonuses and special benefits, and report-auditing.

ORGANIZATIONAL INTERVENTIONS

Many leaders try to bring about change in organizations by administrative changes. Memos are sent or wages and rewards are manipulated. Sending a memo to the effect that a certain behavior will begin or end at a specified time can backfire.

> Jane Warden, Assistant Director of Nursing, noticed nursing staff were wasting toilet paper in their rest rooms. She sent a memo that as of that day staff were to be more conservative of supplies. Following the memo, toilet paper waste increased. The staff viewed the memo as a challenge and another sign of being treated as irresponsible children. A whole series of strategy-counterstrategies were played out until Jane decided the use of toilet paper was taking up too much time for its level of priority. She stopped mentioning the item and toilet paper useage dropped to its level prior to the first memo.

Some studies of productivity have demonstrated that money incentives are not as important as time incentives, that improving personnel selection methods decreases labor turnover, and that accidents on the job are reduced more by increasing the degree of comfort in the work environment than by providing rewards or threats. (Rothe, 1960; Fleishman & Berniger, 1960; Kennan, Kerr, & Sherman, 1951)

Dyer (1976, p. 93) says the following interventions can affect system output variables:

1. *Social System*
   - Involve workers in setting goals and making decisions.
   - Keep people informed about what is happening in the system.
   - Open communications between all workers.
   - Develop a high level of trust and acceptance.
   - Keep both person-centered and task-centered orientations.
   - Set high performance goals.
   - Convey the idea that workers are needed, useful, and doing something worthwhile in their work.
   - Develop team spirit.
   - Teach supervisors to provide support and recognition.
   - Help workers and supervisors identify areas where additional help is needed.
   - Refrain from exerting undue pressure on workers.

2. *Operation System*
   - Provide an opportunity for workers to use a variety of skills.
   - Match the requirements of the work to the personal resources of workers.
   - Allow time for workers to interact with one another and build support groups.
   - Ensure physical conditions are comfortable, safe, and excess work is not required.
   - Make workers responsible for the quality of output.
   - Ensure that there are not too many conflicting interfaces with other systems.

3. *Administrative System*
   - Base promotions on open review between supervisor and supervisee.
   - Delegate authority and responsibility appropriately.
   - Distribute benefits equitably.
   - Ensure policies and procedures; do not restrict development of the social system.
   - Establish rules and regulations jointly with workers whenever feasible.
   - Encourage workers to collaborate with management to set goals and plan work.
   - Avoid using restrictive reporting and auditing as control measures.
   - Allow for modification in procedures and rules.
   - Formally reward appropriate behavior in managers and workers.

To maximize quality output from workers, all three systems must be mutually reinforcing. It will help to work on one or another system; but the best results will be obtained by building a mutually reinforcing organization.

It is not unusual to hear nurse leaders ask, "What can I do to motivate my staff?" Goren and Ottaway (1985) suggest that many health care teams do not change and appear motivated because of organizational chronicity and collusion. Seemingly unchangeable problem behavior is maintained by the unacknowledged support of the system and because solutions often add to the problem.

Team members rarely admit to supporting the problem solution and tend to scapegoat one individual ("he isn't doing his job") or a subsystem ("physicians are little gods around here"). The physician can not be authoritarian unless the nurse is passive and acquiescent. The individual who slacks off does so because his coworkers take up the slack.

Often team members want a problem solved, but prefer not to change. Instead, they prefer to make their usual behavior more effective. Often, this is impossible. For example, team members may need to learn to take the responsibility for speaking up and being assertive and to take the risk related to how that change may affect the system.

Organizations may not change for a variety of reasons, including:

1. Leaders and workers collude (or unconsciously agree) not to change. Any of the following can be unconsciously agreed upon decisions that can hamper productivity and goal achievement: vague and unmeasurable goals, unachievable goals, incongruent goals (the director of nursing wants to prevent unionization and the staff wants the director of nursing to change her leadership style), or goals that are incongruent with the available options. "Collusion is the result of trying to achieve success without enduring the pain and difficulty of change" (Goren and Ottaway, 1985, p. 11). Nurse leaders may collude with their staff by publicly valuing a behavior, but secretly valuing another. These hidden agendas will prevent change because lip service will not be sufficient to induce change. It may delude nurse leaders into believing they are making the effort, but no one else is.

2. Staff development and/or other administrators act on the idea that change occurs by sending "troublemakers" for

training. This is problematic because those sent for training are not motivated to change and probably will not. It is also problematic because even if a few staff do change, once they return to their work system, new behaviors will be treated as deviant and pressure will be exerted to return to old behavior patterns. An organizational change program must be one that is mutually agreed upon and entered in to by all organizational members.

3. Solutions are focused on understanding the problem rather than changing it. This is evident when the following types of comments are made: "How did we get this way?" "How did this happen?" "Let's see if we can understand the problem." (These kinds of comments focus on insight and history; questions more effective in guiding change are: "How does having this problem maintain the system?" and "What can be done about it?")

4. Competition rather than collaboration is fostered. Nurse leaders who want change must make that expectation clear to staff and must provide the tools and skills needed to effect change. Rewards must be given for collaboration, if collaboration is to occur. For example, publicly acknowledging an ability to teach supportive behaviors to other staff would enhance collaboration, while publicly praising a unique ability of one staff member would enhance competition.

THE NURSE EXECUTIVE'S ROLE IN CHANGE

Byers (1984a) has examined the nurse executive's role in organizational change, and suggests the following seven steps in clarifying this emerging role:

1. Explain and interpret nursing as a clinical practice discipline in the organizational contexts of planning forums, marketing program, financial management, and clinical care programs.

2. Participate in executive management by providing input and influence regarding policy and strategic planning decisions.
3. Establish internal and external relationships that support clinical nursing practice.
4. Speak about clinical nursing practice using the language of business and organizations.
5. Develop a perspective of nursing practice that separates clinical practice from the organizational elements of support services, marketing, and finance.
6. Establish a data base that promotes organizational understanding of nursing for decision making related to nursing practice.
7. Develop an attitude that nurse administrators and managers *can* work with you, that workers can learn new skills and habits, can be trusted, and will put their efforts where they will make the most difference.

Nurse executives are innovators who participate in strategic planning. They look beyond current needs to envision the future, deal with problems to create better systems, and plan to meet long-term goals developed through study and deliberation (Byers, 1984a). Clearly, nurse executives do not function by jumping from crisis to crisis. They must take time from daily operations to develop a long-range view of nursing. An evaluation of the nursing division provides data needed to analyze its strengths, weaknesses, and potential.

The nurse executive also participates in the trend toward decentralization, by assisting head and staff nurses to accept increased accountability. The executive role may include teaching nurses how to make more complex decisions that are required of them when the layer of supervision is removed.

In line with the perception that nursing is a clinical discipline, is the upgrading of qualifications of the nursing staff toward the utilization of registered nurses. The organizational structure may need to be changed in order to upgrade the nursing staff. A different kind of organizational support is needed to assist professional nurses to reintegrate managerial and clinical functions. This reintegration is related to the development of primary nursing as the organizational mode of nursing care delivery. Because the primary nurse functions as a case manager, the nurse executive may need to develop a clinical advancement program or clinical ladder and place clinical specialists in strategic places to provide guidance and education for staff nurses as well as provide direct client care. Nursing research findings are used to determine essential nursing care and guide development of programs meeting client needs in outpatient and home settings. The nurse executive participates in developing information systems, including computerized classification systems, nursing staffing protocols, and transmittal of client care orders.

POWER AND POLITICS IN ORGANIZATIONS

Organizations are composed of people who are constantly vying with one another for power, status, and prestige. Information, resources, and support are the commodities necessary for accumulating power. Successful managers often have to overstep the limits of their formal positions; power helps them do this. Power is rarely, if ever, given; it must be taken. Others must be convinced to go along with the manager's ideas. *Coalitions* must be formed during which there is a temporary joining of individuals with a common purpose or goal formed to exert pressure on others. Space, personnel, support, or ideas can be traded to develop power. Posturing or bluffing are used to provide power; more is asked than is ever expected, creating fallback positions. Posturing is an attempt to keep others off balance or keep them guessing about what is expected. Participation in committees, task forces, social gatherings, or special projects of powerful individuals increases visibility and increases the possibility of being seen in the right place at the right time.

Those who are politically vulnerable or expendable are those who get set up and blamed, becoming organizational scapegoats. Politically astute nurse leaders may wish to consider using some or all of the following skills and tactics to increase power (Del Bueno, 1986):

- Build a team, being careful there are not disgruntled, disappointed, or jealous subordinates on it.
- Choose your second in command carefully; agressive, ambitious, or upwardly mobile workers may seize power.
- Establish alliances with both superiors and peers.
- Establish both upward and downward channels of communication; without them, an executive may become isolated and subject to being ousted or preempted.
- Be aware of powerful people's biases; this is crucial to predicting how a decision will be made; decisions rarely stand on their merit alone.
- Identify priorities for the organization and follow them; three kinds of routines found in organizations are: survival tasks done to protect self and position, camouflage routines done to disguise the use of survival routines, and task routines.
- Identify when to be fair; being fair to aggressive manipulative individuals may lead to a takeover of one's power or job.
- Be courteous; when others feel good or powerful, they will not have a need to retaliate.
- Compromise on small issues and only have a few issues that are ethically or morally essential; this will provide a flexible position and maneuverability.
- Use passive resistance when under pressure to perform on demands that cannot be openly challenged, yet are not in one's best interests.

- Project an image of power, status, and material success; others may mistake modesty and democracy for lack of power and influence.
- Divert an organized attack by initiating internal dissension or introduce an issue or rumor that sets your adversaries fighting among themselves.

Del Bueno (1986) points out that women may try to rise above power plays and politics; this may lead to being left out of important decisions. Nurse leaders must identify and learn to play the games their organization plays if they hope to develop power.

Coplin, O'Leary and Gould (1985, pp. 5–17) suggest the following steps for predicting and influencing the outcome of a decision in a group or organization:

1. Define the decision to be forecast.
2. Identify every major player in the organization who can affect the outcome.
3. Assess the extent to which each player supports or opposes the decision (their position). Use $+5$ as support, -5 as opposition, and 0 as neutrality.
4. Assess the extent to which each player can influence the decision (their power).
5. Assess the amount of importance each player places on the outcome of the decision (the priority).
6. Determine the probability that a favorable decision will be made by dividing the sum of positive scores by the sum of absolute value of all scores.
7. Use the information to convince decision makers to side with you.
8. When players do not support your moves, work early and hard to either slow down the decision (call for more study, suggest wider collaboration, urge that more information be gathered, point out that outside consultants could provide valuable insights) or speed it up to maximize current support (argue that enough

time has already been spent on the decision, point out outside consultants wouldn't be able to understand the problem, suggest that a decision be made by the small group of players familiar with the decision, urge that information gathered by surveys can be misleading).

9. Change players' positions by using reason ("logic and evidence dictate it"), guilt ("you owe it to me."), love ("if you loved me . . ."), fear (". . . or there's no telling what might happen."), power ("if you do that, I'm sure you'll understand how unhappy we'll all be"), promises ("if you do this for me, I'll . . .), authority ("it's your job to support me"), forecasting ("it's inevitable anyway"), friendship ("what's this between friends?"), history ("it's happened this way before").

10. Increase legitimacy by being associated with winning decisions, becoming a master of scarce information, or hiring someone to do public relations (e.g., tell important others how an outside competitor is eager to hire you).

READINGS

Byers, M. (1984a). Getting on top of organizational change: Part 2. Trends in nursing service. *Journal of Nursing Administration* *14* (11), 31–37.

Byers, M. (1984b). Getting on top of organizational change: Part 3. The corporate nurse executive. *Journal of Nursing Administration* *14* (12), 32–37.

Cavanaugh, D. (1985). Gamesmanship: The art of strategizing. *Journal of Nursing Administration 15* (4), 38–41.

Coplin, W., O'Leary, M., & Gould, C. (1985). *Power persuasion.* Reading MA: Addison-Wesley.

Del Bueno, D. (1986). Power and politics in organizations. *Nursing Outlook 34* (3), 124–128.

Dyer, W. (1976). *Insight to impact, strategies for interpersonal and organizational change.* Provo, UT: Brigham Young University.

Ehrat, K. (1983). A model for politically astute planning and decision making. *Journal of Nursing Administration 13* (9), 29–35.

Elpern, E. et al. (1984). Staff governance the experience of one nursing unit. *Journal of Nursing Administration 14* (6), 9–21.

Fleishman, E., & Berniger, J. (1960). One way to reduce office turnover. *Personnel 37*, 63–69.

Glaser, E. (1983). Impact of a quality of worklife (QWL) improvement effort at a mental health facility. *Consultation 2 (1)*, 11–17.

Goren, S. & Ottaway, R. (1985). Why health-care teams don't change. Chronicity and collusion. *Journal of Nursing Administration 15* (7/8) 9–16.

Haffer, A. (1986). Facilitating change, choosing the appropriate strategy. *Journal of Nursing Administration 16* (4), 18–22.

Jacobsen-Webb, M. (1985). Team building: Key to executive success. *Journal of Nursing Administration 15* (2), 16–20.

Keenan, V., Kerr, W., & Sherman, W. (1951). Psychological climate and accidents in an automotive plant. *Journal of Applied Psychology 35*, 89–91.

Lamar, E. (1985). Communicating personal power through nonverbal behavior, *Journal of Nursing Administration 15* (1), 41–44.

McClure, M. (1984). Managing the professional nurse: Part 1. Organizational theories. *Journal of Nursing Administration 14* (2), 15–21.

Peterson, M. (1986). Shared governance: A strategy for transforming organizations. Part 1. *Journal of Nursing Administration 16* (1), 9–12.

Porter-O'Grady, T. (1985). Credentialing, privileging, and nursing bylaws assuring accountability. *Journal of Nursing Administration 15* (12), 23–27.

Roth, H. (1960). Does higher pay bring higher productivity? *Personnel 37*, 20–27.

Smith, H. et al. (1984). Japanese management implications for nursing administration. *Journal of Nursing Administration 14* (9), 33–39.

Weiczorek, R. (Ed.) (1985). *Power, politics and policy in nursing*. New York: Springer.

10
When the Community is the Group

COMMUNITY ORGANIZATION

Community organization is the process of building a broad-based constituency, involving citizens in a program, or creating a new, community-based program. Support for a program will logically emerge if community needs and concerns are understood and focused upon. Sometimes, issues for community organization surface naturally. The nurse group leader must be ready to mobilize the community around the issue of concern, set a meeting to discuss the situation, and involve the community's leaders to build momentum for programs. Community members often have different goals than nurses; it is often necessary to work on community issues as defined by the community in order to develop a meaningful organizational structure. Discussing drug or alcohol abuse or prevention of hazardous situations may be irrelevant to community members until they recognize the need for intervention.

Bevins (1979, p. 127) identified the following characteristics necessary for the nurse group leader who plans to attempt community organization:

- Solid training by others who have successfully practiced community organization
- Self-assurance and willingness to try new things

- Enthusiasm
- Good judgment
- An abiding belief in people and that informed citizens can find the right answers—a belief in democracy
- Willingness to subordinate personal opinions to informed, collective judgments of community members
- Refusal to manipulate others
- Willingness to visit people to learn their feelings, to inform them of what others are saying, and to assure them that they are not powerless
- Willingness to do the needed organizational background work and let citizen leaders take center stage
- Confidence that the inevitable barriers that emerge can be overcome
- A sense of humor
- A capacity for enjoying people and the constantly changing process, and an ability to communicate this good will

Bevins (1979, pp. 127–128) listed the following elements of community organization for health:

- Thorough knowledge of the health problems of the community including target groups and persons at highest risk
- Thorough knowledge of the racial composition, businesses, labor composition, age levels, schools and other institutions, organizations, resources, power groups, traditional community action patterns, and patterns of communication
- Identification of elected and natural leaders
- Identification of natural neighborhoods
- Opinion surveys conducted person-to-person and informally by solicitious individuals
- Broad communication of the results of the opinion surveys
- Organization of concerned groups to discuss identified problems

- Emergence of a highly representative planning group to establish priority goals from the opinions expressed in the survey
- General acceptance of the goals and action plans by all neighborhood groups involved
- Development of neighborhood committees
- Training of volunteers
- Utilization of all possible neighborhood resources
- Frequent meetings of neighborhood and central planning groups
- Consistent feedback to community residents
- Utilization of media
- Development of needed educational materials
- Appropriate documentation of actions
- Public credit for productive leaders
- Maintained momentum
- Willingness to try new approaches if the planned ones do not work
- Communication of results and successes
- Movement to second priority goal once first priority has been attained.

At times, the nurse group leader may need to identify issues by drawing attention to existing community problems and providing statistics that may generate enough concern to bring community members to a meeting to discuss ways of addressing the problem.

Strong grassroots community organizations rarely spring up spontaneously. The nurse group leader may talk to community members informally for months before sufficient concern is generated to warrant a meeting. A crisis situation like a death or major injury is often the focus for immediate mobilization; the nurse group leader must seize the moment when a crisis occurs and use it to mobilize community members.

Another useful way of involving the community is by developing a neighborhood festival or health fair. Many health issues involve (or should involve) children. Therefore, the community-minded nurse group leader must gain access to public schools. Schools in some communities, often in low-income ones, have developed adversary relationships with community groups and may resist school–community partnerships. One way to develop a working relationship with a school is to meet with the principal. If the principal is known to be antagonistic to community groups, the school's parent group can be approached first and asked to support a meeting with the principal. Sympathetic teachers are another group that can be approached for initial contact.

It may be difficult to involve members of low-income communities; they may be too concerned with survival needs to respond to long-term planning. It is wise to seek out a few parents with potential for becoming strong community leaders and concentrate efforts on making sufficient home visits to cajole them to attend or sponsor community meetings. The nurse group leader must become familiar with information networks and natural helpers in a community, including: well-known house wives and service providers such as post office workers, barbers, hairdressers, grocers, pharmacists, religious leaders, and elderly citizens. (Resnik, 1980)

Network building is an essential skill for the nurse group leader. Interagency rivalries must be identified and defused. The following principles are suggested (Resnik, 1980):

- Identify modest aims and demands; agencies are more likely to support a network if they are not greatly inconvenienced by it.
- Clearly specify goals and purposes.
- Avoid spending more time on interagency coordination and networking than on each agency doing its respective job.

- Develop networks around specific needs and opportunities; avoid general goals.
- Develop networks so that participants can see a tangible payoff for their efforts.
- Ensure that the network takes community members' needs into account.

COMMUNITY ASSESSMENT

A community assessment provides the nurse group leader with information about a community's needs, unique character and flavor, its leadership and communication networks, and its culture and history. The process of needs assessment can also bring the nurse group leader and the community closer together, thus developing mutual respect and trust.

Traditionally, a *needs assessment* is a systematic survey of a community's social, political, economic, and demographic composition. Problems and variables related to the issues a program will address are also assessed. A community assessment has two components: process (the various methods used to collect information about the community) and product (a report that summarizes community needs).

On the surface, a needs assessment appears scientifically objective. However, biases can creep in. The kind of information sought implies a set of assumptions about both the problems the community wishes to deal with and ways of solving them. One way to protect against bias is to openly recognize that biases and assumptions exist and try to balance them by examining a wide variety of community variables.

In middle-class communities, the nurse group leader may be able to rely heavily on data collected by community surveys, the juvenile justice system, the census bureau, the schools, and similar human service agencies. In low-income communities, residents are often involved in adversary relationships with agencies so that their data may be highly biased.

In low-income communities, residents may be highly suspicious of anyone who plays an investigating or questioning role. One way of overcoming this obstacle is for teams of nurses or staff members to select streets or blocks in the community and go door to door, introducing themselves and asking for an opportunity to describe the kinds of services they offer. This method enables the staff to gather information as well as to provide it. Community forums focused on discussing and prioritizing community needs have been found useful by the National Indian Board on Alcoholism and Drug Abuse (1979).

In a low-income community, a wide range of formal and informal community information networks must be accessed. These include the official leaders (church leaders, school officials, civic leaders, law enforcement and court officials, representatives of the media, and elected officials), as well as leaders that emerge in school yards, parks, church gatherings, social gatherings, nightclubs, bars, pool halls, and street corners (Wheeler, 1977).

Dyson (1986) suggests helping communities develop neighborhood health watches similar in structure to neighborhood crime watches. He contends that public tabulations on arrests, abortions, teen pregnancies, divorces, school dropouts, and truancy citations become public several months after actual events. "Measuring neighborhood illness rates shows up *quackery,* which I define as spending private and public resources for health without asking what good is obtained" (Dyson, 1986, p. 3).

One of the issues of such a program is confidentiality and privacy. Dyson agrees that privacy must be preserved, but insists there are nonpublic, hidden tragedies that call for immediate remedial action because they create dangerous family and community imbalances. Some of the hidden tragedies to assess are:

- Inappropriate admission to a nursing home
- Students failing in school
- Job loss
- Arrest
- Injury from assault
- Premature birth
- Infant death
- Chronic illness complications

Dyson (1986, p. 3) suggests that weekly counting visits to identify disability days in a sample of families in each block would give timely local information for addressing local needs. Privacy would have to be protected by keeping names anonymous. Clark (1986) has developed a community assessment focused on community wellness needs (Table 10-1).

TABLE 10-1 Community Assessment

Who and What is the Community?

1. How is space distributed and used? (buildings, crowded areas, natural and physical barriers to social interaction, parks, playgrounds)
2. How safe and healthful are work and school environments? (Are smokers and nonsmokers segregated? Are junkfood and cigarette vending machines highly accessible? Are alternatives offered? Is the use of stairways promoted? Are they accessible? Well lit? Is car pooling encouraged? Is flex-time used to allow employees time to engage in wellness activities before work or during lunch? Are high-quality child care services available for residents? Are buildings well-ventilated and have adequate natural light and sufficient work/learning space?)
3. What are the cultural mix and stability of the population? (Are there one or more cultural groups living in harmony or in conflict, and how much acculturation and stress occur due to people moving in or out of the area?)
4. What are the community's age, sex, and family groupings like? (elderly population, single-occupancy commuter group, young-marrieds with children, singles, a mix)

5. What income levels are represented and to what extent? (wealthy, middle-class, poor who receive governmental or charitable assistance for health care, or a mix)
6. What are the occupational levels? (Are they hard-driving executives who leave the family's health concerns to their wives, action-oriented population who <u>learns</u> by doing, a mix? What does the occupational level tell you about the population's education, health problems, problem-solving patterns, and methods of learning?)
7. What community resources are available and where are they? (Where are the schools, hospitals, shopping areas, and clinics located in relation to available transportation? What self-help or supportive groups and services exist in the community? What facilities are there for wellness programs? What space could be developed to provide further wellness services? What skills or resources do the residents have that could be shared through a wellness program exchange? Is there any way to trade unused sick leave for a well day? Could unused sick leave be converted to cash? Do faculty, bosses, or town legislators support personal health promotion objectives? Can additional rewards or incentives be built into the current health/illness insurance programs without taking away existing benefits? If there are company- or school-subsidized cafeterias, could wellness-promoting foods be more subsidized than junk foods?)

How are Needs Met?

1. Are needs met or prevented from being met by space, culture, age, sex, family, income, occupation level, or community resource factors?
2. What do the community's clergy, health care practitioners, welfare agencies, and clients know about what needs are not being met?
3. What do records of health services, worker's compensation claims, and accident and safety records tell you about how needs are met and what wellness needs are not being met?
4. What do questionnaire or survey methods tell you about what community residents say the type of wellness activities they would participate in if offered?
5. What specific risk factors exist in this population and how are they being addressed or not?
6. How can family members of community residents be considered in planning wellness programs and used to provide needed support systems?

(continued)

TABLE 10-1 (*continued*)

How are Deviance and Disturbance Handled?

1. Are those with psychiatric/mental health difficulties rejected by the community? In what way?
2. How are homosexuals; delinquents; or those who abuse alcohol, drugs, or food treated by community members?
3. What political, educational, or social views lead to rejection of those who deviate from the norm?
4. Are there humane or highly institutionalized agencies available in the community to help deal with deviant members? What are they?
5. Does the community reject the idea of placing treatment facilities for its deviants within the community? How?
6. Is there a prevailing view that people who deviate from accepted behavioral patterns should be punished? How is this belief put into practice?

How are Identities Developed?

1. How do families, faculty, administrators, etc. teach their members to act?
2. What kinds of religious/spiritual organizations or groups exist in the community and what is their prevailing view of human motivation?
3. What youth agencies/helpers are there and how do young people relate to them?
4. What kind of formal and special education programs are available and how are they used by the community?
5. How could already existing agencies or groups be used more effectively?

How are Community Functions Accomplished?

1. Are community decisions made before adequate information has been obtained? What possible effect(s) might this have?
2. Are decisions made by default, based on the personal concerns of a few, or made by consensus? What are the consequences of this type of decision making?
3. Is communication fragmented and inefficient? How does such communication seem to affect the community?

4. Are communication messages based on a sense of community (we're all in this together) or on stereotypes and the establishment of distance between groups (It's us against them)? What is the effect of both types of communication messages?

5. How accurately does the local media portray information to the community?

6. Are there informal (rumor) communication channels?

7. Are problems solved informally with board and committee meetings used only to record earlier decisions? How might this affect the community or the decision-making process?

8. How are ad hoc, neighborhood, or block associations used in decision making?

9. How readily are newcomers accepted by the community?

10. Is leadership concentrated among a few groups or is it widely distributed in the community?

11. Are there wide vacillations in power or frequent changes in the power base that could affect health planning or treatment?

12. Where is power located, how is it perceived, and how is it used?

13. What overlapping areas and missing links are there in wellness services?

14. What segments in the community are receptive and hostile to outside influence?

15. Is there a sense of trust between community members and leaders?

16. Is there community disintegration? (Has a recent disaster, widespread ill health, extensive poverty, confusion of cultural values, weakening of religious affiliations, extensive migration of new groups, or rapid social change radically affected the community?)

What are the Resistances to Change in this Community?

1. What factors in the system will be affected as a result of a change toward wellness?

2. What forces are operating to inhibit change toward wellness?

3. What information or experiences must precede the change toward wellness?

4. What new procedures or experiences will need to be developed as a result of a movement toward wellness?

5. Who is likely to suffer from the change?

6. How aware are community residents of the need for change?

7. Are community residents sufficiently involved in planning for the change?

(continued)

TABLE 10-1 (*continued*)

---

8. What is the relationship between the change agent and community residents?
9. What past relationship between the change agent and the client might be influencing resistance to change now?
10. How open have community residents been to the introduction of change in the past?
11. How can free and open communication, administrative support of and reward for problem-solving efforts, shared decision making, sufficient time to problem solve, written statements of what the change goals will be, professionalism, concern for long-term planning, cohesiveness among change agents, and feelings of security among residents, timing, and resident confidence in ability to change be enhanced to lower resistance to change?

Copyright, Carolyn Chambers Clark, 1984

EXAMPLES OF COMMUNITY ORGANIZATION EFFORTS

A Rural County Community Organization Example

In 1948, Charlotte Rickman, a health educator, was sent by her State Medical Society to a small rural county in the mountains. Her job was to help the citizens with their health problems. She studied morbidity–mortality data and knew the diseases and accidents leading to death in the county. She needed to know how the citizens felt about their health needs. She saw hundreds of people, heard their opinions, and generated discussion. Sometime before the citizens had started a hospital, but work had been stopped due to lack of funds. It seemed they were interested in continuing with the hospital with space for a local health department.

Ms. Rickman helped form an informal organization to pool ideas and develop strategies. The community held an auction sale to raise money. The hospital was completed and the health department was opened. Citizens brought fresh fruits and vegetables, meat and canned goods to the hospital to provide meals for patients and staff. The project was celebrated on a nationwide program on NBC radio.

A City Community Organization Example

In the 1960s, Nancy Milio was a community health nurse with Detroit's Visiting Nurse Association. The Mom and Tots Center, which the community developed, was completed with Milio's patience and encouragement and based on their ideas. The center was the only building in several blocks left untouched during the burnings and lootings of the July, 1967 riots in Detroit. The community owned the center and it was not sacrificed, despite the fury and frustration of the time. Her book, *9226 Kercheval—The Storefront That Did Not Burn* (1971), describes in detail the process of community organization Milio set in motion in Detroit.

An Urban-Rural Community Organization Example

Eugenia Sloan was the health educator of the Forsyth County Health Department in 1975. She studied the health statistics for the county and learned that deaths from heart disease and stroke were abnormally high, especially among black males. Ms. Sloan visited the 13 communities, learning who the leaders were, what the available resources were, what institutions and organizations had been established, and how communication occurred. She found the communities distrusted each other.

She helped develop a central committee composed of representatives of the 13 communities. The committee studied the health concerns revealed in the survey and chose heart disease as a focus for education and action. Strong leadership was evident in a group of senior citizens in one community who were especially interested in combating heart disease. Ms. Sloan began working with this small group plus a few other leaders in the area. Natural communication channels were used to spread information about the project.

Goals and objectives were set by the group and activity steps were suggested. The first step was to educate the senior citizens group about factors associated with heart disease. Educational literature was distributed to the community and cardiovascular screenings were conducted by public health nurses at a church well attended by residents of that community.

Screenings were followed up when a citizen learned how to take blood pressure and volunteered to take them regularly at the community house. The community house managers became interested and requested funds for the purchase of blood pressure monitoring equipment. Cuffs and sphygmomanometers were ordered and paid for with housing project funds.

All house managers were certified to screen for hypertension by a physician and public health nurse. Outreach screenings began and forms from the screening were collected by Ms. Sloan and the community house supervisors for evaluation. Periodic problem-solving meetings were also held.

Throughout the participating communities, community house managers continued to screen for blood pressure and to refer for diagnosis those with two unsatisfactory readings. Problems of transportation emerged, but were solved by the project leaders. A great deal of unsuspected hypertension was found and treatment begun. Weight-watching classes and stop-smoking groups were established. Informal discussions in the community houses centered around good nutrition and the best ways to get the most for the food dollar. A feeling of empowerment occurred in the 13 formerly helpless communities. Other needs were identified as important, including more recreation areas and equipment, better houses, better means of communication with others, and youth activities.

READINGS

Bevins, E. (1979). Community Organization, An Old But Reliable Health Education Technique. In P. Lazes (Ed.). *The handbook of health education* (pp. 109–130). Germantown, MD: Aspen Systems.

Clark, C. C. (1986). Community wellness programs. In *Wellness nursing: concepts, theory, research and practice*. New York: Springer.

Conroy, G., & Brayer, H. (1978). *Teen involvement for drug abuse prevention: Administrator's guide*. Rockville, MD: National Institute of Drug Abuse.

Dyson, B. (April, 1986). Measuring neighborhood health. *The Network 12*, 2–3.

Green, L. et al. (1980). *Health education planning: A diagnostic approach*. Palo Alto, CA: Mayfield Publishing.

Milio, N. (1971). *9226 Kercheval: The storefront that did not burn*. Ann Arbor, MI: University of Michigan Press.

National Indian Board on Alcoholism and Drug Abuse. (1979). *Needs assessment in Indian communities*. Tempe, AZ: National Indian Board on Alcoholism and Drug Abuse.

Resnik, H. (1980). *Drug abuse prevention for low-income communities: Manual for program planning*. Rockville, MD: National Institute on Drug Abuse.

Wheeler, W. (1977). *Counseling from a cultural perspective*. Atlanta: A. L. Nellum and Associates.

Glossary of Selected
Group Terms

aggressiveness   behavior that has an element of control or manipulation of the other person.

anxiety   unexplained feeling of discomfort that occurs when expectations are not met.

apathy   a withdrawal response that can be used to cover tension and discomfort.

assertiveness   setting goals, acting on those goals in a clear and consistent way, and taking responsibility for the consequences of those actions.

behavior description   a statement of what was observed, without including a comment on the meaning or motive for the behavior.

behavioral modification   an approach to change that focuses on principles of learning, such as reinforcement, that can decrease unsatisfying or disruptive behavior and on increasing satisfying, goal-directed behavior.

closed group   a group to which new members are not added when others leave.

coalition   a temporary joining of individuals with a common purpose or goal formed to exert pressure on others.

cohesiveness   the measure of attraction of the group for its members.

community organization the process of building a broader-based constituency, involving citizens in a program, or creating a new, community-based program.

countertransference leader response in an over- or underreactive way to group members because they evoke remembrances of earlier personal relationships of the leader.

covert content the deeper, symbolic meaning of words.

feedback letting group members know how they affect each other.

group conflict reaction to being given an impossible task, having contradictory loyalties, jockeying for power or status, disliking others, or involving oneself in the task.

group contract a written or verbal operating agreement between leader and group members.

group event behavior of all group members except the designated leader.

group process constant movement as group members seek to reduce the tension that arises when people attempt to have their individual needs met yet work to help meet group goals.

hidden agenda individual member or leader goals that are at cross-purposes to group goals.

"I" messages verbal communication that conveys the way the individual thinks or feels.

incompatible response one that cannot be performed at the same time as the desired behavior.

maintenance functions those that are directly related to improving interpersonal relationships within the group.

manipulation attempt by group member to have his own needs met.

modeling   demonstrating desired behaviors.

monopolizing   a group problem wherein one group member agrees in some way with other group members to talk and thereby to protect them.

needs assessment   a systematic survey.

norm   rule for behavior in the group.

open group   a group to which new members can be added as others drop out.

organizational system   composed of the social system, operation system and administrative system of an organization.

orientation phase   early group phase when anxiety is high, levels of self-disclosure are low, bids for the leader's attention or care are made, group goals are refined, and the leader models effective group behavior.

overt content   superficial, agreed-upon meaning of words.

pairing   behavior whereby group members pair off in twos to provide mutual support for one another through having subconversations; characteristic of the orientation phase.

prompting   telling a person how to behave next.

reinforcers   rewarding events that immediately follow a behavior and thus maintain its occurrence.

resistance   phenomenon that occurs when people fear change or lack knowledge of or participation in the change.

scapegoating   a group process wherein one or two members of the group are singled out and agree consciously or unconsciously to be targets for group hostility or advice.

shaping   the reinforcement of successive approximations toward the desired behavior.

silence   a communication that has various meanings.

supportive group a group whose main purpose is to share thoughts, feelings, and reactions to crises, health conditions, or interpersonal relationships.

task functions those that are directly related to the accomplishment of group goals.

task group a group with a main purpose of completing a task.

teaching group a group whose main purpose is to impart information.

termination phase the last phase, wherein the group focuses on evaluating and summarizing the group experience.

themes linkages and underlying consistent meaning in group interaction.

time out removing the person from a pleasurable activity immediately, once undesirable behavior occurs.

token system symbolic reward for desirable behavior that can be turned in at a later date for more concrete rewards.

transference member response whereby aspects of former relationships are projected onto current figures in the group setting.

validating checking with the other in a tentative way to see whether one's perceptions are correct.

warming-up exercises exercises used to decrease group anxiety.

working phase the middle phase in a group, when members know how to work together cooperatively, thoughts and feelings are shared more openly, and the leader needs to intervene less frequently to move the group along.

"You" message aggressive verbal communication in which blame is placed on the other person.

Index